SECRETS FROM THE LOST ART OF COMMON SENSE MARKETING

D0360384

Illustrated by James H. Jukes
Cover Design by Dan Carlson
Color Processing by Ted Willett

H. Brad Antin   Alan J. Antin

Dedication

We dedicate this book to our father, Sid Antin, an uncommon man who first taught us the value of common sense, and continues to teach us even now.

Thanks dad...

Also, to Gary Halbert. A friend and sounding board who tells us what we need to know even if it's not what we want to hear.

Secrets From The Lost Art Of Common Sense Marketing

Preface

The economic environment is a reflection of the marketplace. It's a reflection of how the population thinks and feels, and right now, they feel lousy and they think the worst.

The economic climate is also a reflection of where we've been. But the important thing is that if you look, I mean really look, and think about it, it will tell you where we're going.

And for the 90's and beyond, the sign posts point in a totally new direction.

You see, the underlying values of American society, our basic fundamental national psyche, are undergoing an evolution unlike anything we've ever before seen.

The business that understands this
change and reacts to it will prosper.

The key to success for American business in the future lies not in imitating the past, but in understanding and learning from it.

Those who ignore these fundamental changes and simply wait for the economy to turn around will wither and die.

Most businesses got caught up in the glitz and excesses of the 80's. For many, the 80's were *"boom years;"* a decade which gave birth to more new businesses than any other time in our history.

In the case of many of today's small and mid-sized businesses, the 80's were *all they knew*. They grew up in a business climate that relied on paper profits, leveraged buy outs, easy credit, and other artificial growth aids.

Doing business in the 80's was like body building with steroids. All we thought of was the *"quick fix"* and the *"fast buck."* Everyone knew that down the road there would be a price to pay, but nobody wanted to think about it, so we just ignored it... Until our economy (and our businesses) got sick.

Perhaps we should have called this book:
"*First Aid For Your Ailing Business.*"

Just as the freewheeling 80's was the decade of steroids, the sobering 90's are already telling us that we need a period of healing, a return to the wise old "*back-to-basics*" remedies that have worked throughout the ages.

"*The Lost Art Of Common Sense Marketing*" is that "*back-to-basics*" remedy. Use it to cure the problems plaguing your business right now, and in the future.

If you aren't convinced that you need to make some changes, look around and notice how many big businesses are laying off workers by the thousands.

How many of these newly unemployed workers were you counting on to be your customers?

In 1992, GM announced plans to shut down 21 plants. How many of these plants would you have supplied with equipment, materials, or services?

When business fails to respond
to the marketplace, the marketplace
stops doing business.

And that has a trickle-down effect on every business. In fact, it has an effect on all of us. It's not just a problem for "big business" either. Every day, dozens of medium and small businesses are also closing their doors.

If you still doubt that fundamental changes are taking place... changes that will significantly affect you and your business... changes unlike any you've seen before, consider this...

The current recession (as of this writing, early 1992), is not a bad one as far as the numbers show. The economic output of the country is not nearly as low as it's been in past recessions. Unemployment is not as high as during other recessions (7% now, versus 11% in 1982). But the confidence factor, the way people feel, is at it's lowest point in decades.

According to Faith Popcorn, noted trend forecaster, futurist, and author of the best-selling book, "*The Popcorn Report*"...

American attitudes are changing.

In their desire to avoid the harsh realities of the outside world, and their mile-a-minute, almost schizophrenic lives, American consumers are "*digging in*" and "*cashing out.*"

They're nostalgically looking for the "*good old days,*" or trying to escape to a real world "*fantasy island*" without even leaving the comfort of home. They can no longer afford every new luxury, so they're rewarding themselves with smaller, more affordable indulgences.

They're no longer willing to settle for just being a "*number,*" and they're demanding more personalized attention from the businesses they patronize.

A new social conscience is stirring. Ethics, passion, service, compassion, and basic honesty are "*in,*" and hype, glitz and moral bankruptcy are "*out.*"

Consumers are "mad as hell, and they're not gonna take it any more."

If you don't pay attention... If you don't adapt...

If you don't wake up and do something right now, you might not get another chance.

This is not simply just a case of "*the little boy who cried wolf.*" Right now, the big bad wolf is roaming your flock, and one-by-one, he is slowly eating your sheep. If you don't take action, your flock may soon be gone.

It's our sincere desire to help you make a few changes in your business that will not only add tremendously to your bottom line, but could, quite literally, mean the difference between its life and death.

Most businesses in this country are suffering, and that's tragic, but the real tragedy is that the business owners are blaming the economy for problems they themselves have been creating for years.

And now, they're paying the price.

They know that times are tough, and they should do something about plummeting sales figures, but they simply haven't got a clue as to what that something should be.

Many of them are simply moping around the office or the store, *pretending* to be doing something.

Imagine a deer on the highway staring into the bright lights of an oncoming car: paralyzed, afraid to make a move, until... Well, you know how that turns out.

The same is true with a business that becomes paralyzed. Only instead of being struck by a car, people call it "*death by recession*".

The sad truth of the matter is that it should really be called suicide!

"Unintentional" suicide maybe, but it's suicide just the same.

Most of these businesses could have been easily saved, but their owners based too many important decisions on the past, rather than on the future.

We're not trying to talk you out of the recession. We're not going to tell you that it's a matter of mental attitude, or that "*The recession is just a state of mind.*"

The recession is quite real, and it will take its toll on even the best run businesses. But, you should know that this recession is actually just a symptom, not the real disease.

Most of the businesses that recognize this and make the proper adjustments could come out of it quite well. Better, in fact, than when the recession started.

We won't tell you that every business *can* survive. Some of them can't.

But we will tell you that almost any business, with the right corrective action, *could* survive.

You see, the problem with most businesses lies more in the mistakes they've been making for years (or in the case of a new business, from the beginning), than with the recession.

The recession is merely "*the straw that broke the camel's back.*"

Granted, it reduces the pool of available new customers.

Granted, it lowers demand for your product or services.

But there is still plenty of business to be had. The recession will mostly cost you the easy sales. You know, "*the gravy.*"

The secrets contained in this book will show you how to recover those lost sales and more. In fact, since most of your competitors are in the same boat as you, making the proper corrections now will help you grab far more market share from them than you are losing to the recession.

And when the recession ends, watch out! You'll be amazed at the compounding effects of these corrections. The profits will be absolutely staggering!

Introduction:
Your Business, Marketing, and The Lost Art Of Common Sense

Are you a retailer? A wholesaler? Or, perhaps a restaurateur?

Do you provide some kind of service such as dry cleaning or house painting?

Or, are you a doctor, lawyer, or some other professional?

Whatever your answer, the first thing you need to understand is that above all else...

You are in the marketing business.

Sure, your product or service may be different than ours, you may sell to different customers than we sell, but no matter what, your business is still a marketing business.

You're not a doctor... *You market medical services.*

You're not a furniture dealer... *You market furniture to consumers.*

You're not a plumber... *You market plumbing services.*

You're not a hard goods distributor... *You market hard goods to dealers.*

This is true without exception; no matter what you sell, how you sell it, or to whom you sell it.

Remember this always, because the moment you lose sight of it, trouble will be just around the corner. There are no if's, and's, or buts. You are in the marketing business.

But what is marketing?

Is it advertising?

Is it how you display your goods?

Is it how often you (or your reps) call on your accounts?

Is it your sales presentation?

Is it the signage in front of your stores?

Is it the cleanliness of you store, shop, or office?

The answer is YES!

Marketing is everything your customer or potential customer sees, hears, smells, feels, tastes, thinks, or even wonders about your business.

Anything that causes the customer to form an impression or just have a thought about your business is marketing.

Marketing is what gets and keeps your customers.

If you do it right, you'll prosper.

If you don't do it right, you may prosper for a while (assuming demand for your product or service is high enough, or your competitors are also doing it wrong), but eventually you'll run into trouble.

You'll see that your entire business is built on a house of cards, and the least little economic "sneeze" could blow it down.

Everything we are about to teach you is predicated on the fact that you at least run an honest business that delivers what you promise. If you don't, you might as well throw this book away right now... The "*secrets*" contained on these pages won't work for you.

You see, the true foundation upon which all great marketing is built is the unselfish desire to do good for your customers. The actual marketing, on the other hand, is simply making sure that they know about it.

In other words, *"If you always do good, (and market properly), you'll always do well."*

Without great customer service, nothing in the world will keep your customers coming back for more... the greatest advertising in the world won't do it... the greatest salesmen in the world won't... even the greatest products in the world won't overcome poor customer service.

That's the harsh reality of today's business climate.

A wise old man (our father) often told us...

"A business has only two functions: to serve it's customers better than anyone else, and to make a profit. If it fails in either one of these functions for any length of time, it will surely perish."

What is "*The Lost Art Of Common Sense Marketing*"?

Simply this! A collection of concepts, techniques, rules, guidelines, and attitudes that can help almost any business to not only survive, but to actually grow and prosper in virtually any economic climate.

Of course, we didn't invent *"The Lost Art Of Common Sense Marketing."* It's been around for ages. We simply *"rediscovered"* the pieces and reassembled them in a way that is easily understood and usable by virtually *any* business.

All of the notes had already been discovered before Mozart wrote his first concerto...

All of the colors had long been discovered before Picasso painted his first canvas...

All of the words had long been written before Shakespeare wrote his first play...

But these masters combined the elements in such a way as to more perfectly communicate their messages.

So it is with *"The Lost Art Of Common Sense Marketing."*

We took the *notes, colors,* and *words* of hundreds of years of history, and combined them with the experiences and teachings of the past masters.

We added to this our own years of trial and error, successes and failures, and over 10,000 hours of intense research.

And then we massaged and worked this mix until we could isolate the most important and effective marketing concepts, techniques, rules, and guidelines in the world.

Finally, we can now present them to you in an easy-to-understand format sure to become one of your most valuable tools for doing business today and in the future.

This book represents just a small sampling of secrets from *"The Lost Art Of Common Sense Marketing."* But don't underestimate what you'll achieve when you apply even just a few of these basics. The results will astound you.

The art of common sense is the uncanny (and altogether too rare) ability to see the obvious.

It's the ability to see the forest *in spite* of the trees.

Most of the *"secrets"* that you're about to learn are truly common sense. They're the types of things that you never think of until someone else points them out to you.

They're the types of things that, once called to your attention, cause you to slap yourself in the head and say: *"That's obvious!"* or, *"I should have known that."* or, *"Why didn't I think of that?"*

In fact, some of these *"secrets"* are so obvious and so simple that you'll swear you already knew them even though you never before gave them a moment's thought.

To tell you the truth, some of them are so painfully simple that I've heard people actually snicker while reading them.

But it's our clients that usually have the last laugh... when they attend the snickerer's "*going out of business*" sale.

The moral...

Just because some of these "secrets" are "as plain as the nose on your face," don't fall prey to underestimating their worth.

The twelve "*secrets*" discussed in this book are the building blocks that every business owner (who wants to survive in the coming years) should use to form the foundation of his or her entire marketing plan.

They'll give you the ability to leverage your marketing efforts to such an extent that you'll probably wonder how you got along without them.

"*The Lost Art Of Common Sense Marketing*" is strong medicine, indeed. And although the dozen "*secrets*" contained and explained in this short book are only the beginning, they do make a potent first dose.

OK, enough preaching.

Now, sit back, relax, and get ready to learn how easily you can use these twelve simple, yet powerful "*secrets*" from "*The Lost Art Of Common Sense Marketing*" to turn your business into a vibrant, healthy, more profitable company for the 90's and beyond!

The First Secret:

Don't Answer Your Own Questions!

One of the most challenging and seemingly difficult tasks facing business owners is selecting the right products, services, and promotions to offer their customers.

In fact, in almost every case, the first thing new clients tell us is that they've tried everything they could think of to generate new business, all to no avail.

They go on to describe promotion after promotion. They show us one new product after another, and they tell us about the multitude of different images they've adopted in order to attract customers.

They tell us how one consultant said "*do this,*" and another consultant said "*do that,*" and yet a third consultant advised something else altogether.

By the time they get to us, they're often completely confused and frustrated. They get that glazed look in their eyes and say something like, "*We've tried everything we could think of, and nothing seems to work. What do my customers want from me, anyway?*"

At about this point in the conversation, we put on our wisest, most "*guru-like*" expressions and prepare to give them the all-important answer that they seek.

We look them right in the eye and one of us says...

"What the hell are you asking me for?
Why don't you ask your customers?"

After all, the only thing that matters is what they want. The only opinions that count are their opinions.

Of course, we weren't always this smart...

Let us tell you how we learned this important secret of *"The Lost Art Of Common Sense Marketing."*

More years ago than we care to remember, (before the lost art got lost), we opened our first business. Like most young entrepreneurs, we were intimately involved with our customers. In fact, we personally talked to almost every single customer who came in.

Well, we didn't know much about business then. So when a customer hinted that some new little service would be nice, or that he wanted something special, we provided it. Not because we were that smart, mind you, but because we wanted the sale.

Back then, when a sales rep came in with some new product that we could offer to our customers, we didn't know what to do, so we asked him to leave a sample or two so we could *"think about it."*

Think about it? Hell, we didn't want to look stupid in front of the sales rep because we didn't even know what questions to ask him.

Anyway, we had some pretty smart customers who always seemed to have good suggestions, so we showed the new product to them. If enough of them liked the new product, we carried it. If not, we didn't.

We weren't even smart enough to make our own buying decisions.

Of course, back then we couldn't afford an ad agency, so we had to design the ads ourselves. And again, since we didn't know what we were doing, we just advertised the products that our existing customers liked.

And since we didn't know what we should say about these products, we just told people what our customers liked about them.

I guess people must have felt sorry for us, because even with these crude, *"Plain-Jane"* advertisements, we kept getting more and more customers.

Somehow, in spite of our inexperience... And even though we didn't know the first thing about marketing... Our business grew.

Well, that's kind of an understatement, because in almost no time, we were generating annual sales of several million dollars.

And then we started believing that WE were the experts.

Before we knew it, we had thirty salesmen servicing customers at five stores. We became a leader in our industry.

By then, we thought we knew *everything*. Pretty soon people from around the country would ask *us* what to carry and how to advertise. And believe me, we had "*all the answers.*"

We no longer needed to ask our customers what to carry. We didn't need to ask them how to advertise. We were experienced. We were successful. We were "**THE EXPERTS.**" At least *we* thought we were.

One day we woke up and noticed that for the first time in our history, sales were dropping a little... and then a little more.

Soon, they seemed to be "*dropping like a rock!*"

Naturally this concerned us, so we hired the most expensive (presumably the best) consultants available.

They said "*do this*," and "*do that*," and "*do the other thing*." But nothing worked.

Sure, we had the answers... But nobody told us that the questions had changed!

We had stopped taking advantage of the very best business consultants that money could buy...

The ones who had helped us in the beginning, before we got so smart...

The ones who really created all of our growth...

We had stopped listening to our own customers!

When your business needs a shot in the arm, or if you need some advice on how to get more customers, the best consultants that money can buy are FREE.

They're your own customers!

How often have you been presented with an idea or product that you dismissed by saying something like *"I know my customers, and they'll never buy that."* Or *"My customers won't pay that much."* Or *"Nobody will pay a premium for faster service."*

Do any of these sound familiar?

What do *You* think?

How do you really know what your customers want (or don't want) unless you ask *them*?

The first step in becoming almost invincible to the effects of recessions (or competitors, for that matter) is to make certain that you are fulfilling the needs and desires of the people who are, or who you want to become, your customers.

Most of the business owners who we talk to never even think to ask their customers what they want from them.

They just go along their merry way, providing the products or services that they *think* their customers want, and then work like hell to convince the customers to buy what they have to sell.

This is wrong, wrong, wrong.

It's like trying to cram a
square peg into a round hole.

Think about it. The only reason that customers do business with you is to fulfill some need or desire that *they* have. They want you to solve some problem in their lives.

Find out what these needs are and fill them better than anyone else, and you'll own your entire market. Your competitors will never know what hit them.

So what needs do your customers want filled? Or, maybe even more importantly... What unmet wants or desires do your customers have that you can fill?

Do they need faster service, or lower prices, or a broader selection from which to make their choices? Or do they want only the top of the line, highest quality goods?

Do they want bargain-basement values? Do they want convenience? Do they want more personalized service? Do they want a longer guarantee, or a more extensive service policy?

Do they want you to be open for more hours each day, or more days per week? Do they want you to stock more variety, or do they want to deal with a specialist? Do they want customized products?

We can't tell you what needs, wants, and desires *your* customers want *you* to fill for them. And by now, you know better than to try and answer that question by yourself. It's time to start asking your customers.

Of course, many of your customers aren't really sure themselves.

But you can bet that they'll know it when they see it, and the day you start fulfilling the right set of needs and desires, you'll be flooded with more new customers than you ever imagined.

You have to start by realizing that you can't be all things to all people. You'll just be diluting your efforts if you try.

But you can (make that *must*) be certain to fill all of the needs that your customers have that are consistent with who you are and what you do.

So how do you find out what they *really* want?

First, talk to your customers, clients, or patients.

No, I really mean *listen* to your customers, clients, or patients!

Ask them why they trade with you. Ask them what they like most (and least) about your company. Ask them if there is any other product or service they would like to see you offer.

Talk to them yourself. After all, you are the one who's responsible.

Try this.

Call a dozen customers on the phone. Tell them that you have a problem, and ask them if they would help you solve it.

Tell them that if they'll give you a few minutes of their time, you'll thank them with some little gift, discount, or bonus.

Tell them that you really want to be the best at what you do, and that you want to know what additional products or services you could offer that would make them happy.

Also, find out what you already do that pleases them the most.

Why did they become your customer in the first place?

Ask them "*If you could have anything you wanted from a (doctor, lawyer, or Indian chief, or whatever your business is), what would it be?*"

Be aware that frequently they'll tell you everything is fine.

But don't give up.

You're placing quite a burden on them by asking them to solve your problem, so make it a little easier.

Ask them "*What is the most frustrating or inconvenient thing about doing business with my company, or any other company in this business?*"

What single thing, no matter how small, bothers them the most about doing business with a _____ (fill in your type of business)?

Next, take it one step further. Ask them about other types of businesses.

Ask them what they hate most about grocery stores, dry cleaners, restaurants, movie rental stores, etc. Frequently, you'll find that important "unmet want" by looking at another industry.

Look for these hidden frustrations and find a way to eliminate them from your business, product, or service.

For example:

A small kitty litter manufacturer, looking for ways to increase their market share, once asked their customers, "*What can we do to improve our product?*" Their customers told them "*Nothing. We love your product the way it is. It works.*"

Not content, the manufacturer then decided to ask their customers what they *disliked* most about kitty litter in general. They heard the obvious... "*I hate having to change it.*" and "*I hate carrying those big bags.*" and "*I hate the smell.*"

But instead of dismissing these remarks as obvious, or saying that's just the way it is, they carefully examined each point. Kitty litter has to be changed, and there's nothing you can do about that.

Economics demands that the only way to give honest value to the customer is to package it in big bags, so they couldn't change that...

But when they evaluated the smell problem, they realized that an obvious improvement had been right under their noses all along.

Soon, this manufacturer became the first to offer scented kitty litter, and their market share virtually exploded.

Their stunned competitors couldn't believe that they had overlooked this *"obvious,"* "common sense" improvement.

When you talk to your customers, listen very carefully, not only to what they say, but to how they say it. Also, pay attention to what they don't say. Read between the lines, and you'll find more answers.

You may need to prompt them a little, but be careful. You don't want to skew their comments.

Get them talking by using open-ended questions. Make them realize that you are truly sincere, and that they have a perspective as a customer that you don't have. And most of all, tell them how much you'd really appreciate their help.

You'll be surprised at what you learn.

Of course, some of them will tell you what they think you want to hear, and some of them will want things that you simply can't deliver, but you'll find a couple of specific things that come up often, which you certainly *can* deliver.

Those are the things that you're looking for.

Once you get this information from your own customers, you're only half way there.

Now you know what you are doing right to attract your existing customers, and you know what you could do better to make these existing customers even happier.

You may even find that you are spending time, effort, and/or money to provide something that doesn't hit your customers' hot buttons.

Here's one area where you can save. If it's not important to your customers, don't do it. For example, if you find that your customers only want bargain-basement merchandise, you don't need to stock much of the higher-end goods.

Don't waste your resources providing what your customers don't care about, but do invest your maximum resources into providing what your customers do want.

What could you offer that would bring you more *new* customers. What could you do to get the customers who are patronizing your competitors, instead of you.

Try this. Run a Contest!

Offer a cash prize or a valuable merchandise prize for the winning entry.

Run an ad with a headline that says something like...

Wanted: Anyone who plans to buy a widget this month! We'll pay you $1,000 for your advice!

My name is Brad Antin. I'm the owner of The Antin Widget Company, and I want to make my company the very best source for widgets in the area.

Most of my customers think that we already provide a great selection and level of service of widgets, but I want to serve you even better.

I was going to hire a fancy consultant to come in, look our business over and tell us what to do to improve it. I'm sure that would help, but then I decided against it.

Here's why. A consultant could tell me ways to run my company more efficiently, or how to display my widgets better, or maybe how to train my salespeople better.

All of that's nice, but it seems to me that the most important thing I can do to improve, is to make absolutely certain that...

We provide you with everything you want from a widget company.

A consultant can only guess at that, and he might guess wrong.

Frankly, I can't afford to take that chance.

So instead of paying a consultant to tell me what he thinks you want, I'd rather pay you to tell me what you want.

That's why I'm running this unusual contest. I'll pay $1,000 in cash to the person who sends in the best suggestion that we can use to improve our company, its products, and services.

Just write down the most important things that we could do to serve you better, and send it to me personally, at the following address.

I'll read every suggestion, and pick the winner. But, since I can only pick one winner, and I'd truly appreciate your help, I'll add a valuable second prize that I'll send to you if you're one of the first 100 entrants.

I'll send each of you a certificate for an instant 20% discount on any widget you'd like.

[Or use a free premium; something else of value.]

Go on to talk about the value of the second prize, and tell them how to respond, etc.

Here's a brilliant concept from "The Reader's Digest"

They know that magazines are an impulse item at the newsstand or check-out counter.

They also know that the only way to trigger the impulse for a reader to pick up (and buy) the magazine is by "*advertising*" the most desired stories on the cover.

But how do they know whether they should promote the new diet on page 45, or the story about a couple who survived a ship-wreck on page 23, or the piece about the new wave of environmentalism on page 67, etc.

**They needed a quick, easy way to find
out exactly what their readers wanted.**

Here's how they did it.

They ran a big ad in newspapers that reached a good cross-section of their typical readers.

In this ad, they listed several of the stories upon which they were working.

They offered to send the reader a special advance copy of any three of these stories absolutely free. All the reader had to do was clip the ad, circle the stories they wanted and send it to "The Reader's Digest."

There were no strings attached. No gimmicks. And no sales pitches.

Well, when "The Reader's Digest" received the responses from the ad, they simply tallied how many copies of each story were requested, and then they knew for sure which of the stories hit the consumers' "*hot-buttons*," and therefore, would generate the most sales.

These are the stories they later advertised on the cover of the magazine.

**Can you imagine what happened to their
newsstand and check-out counter sales next?**

That's right... Through the roof!

All because they took the trouble to find out what their customers really wanted... and delivered it.

How else can you find out what your customers want?

If you're in a retail business, shop your competitors. See for yourself what they do better than you.

Pretend you're one of *their* customers or prospects. See how they handle you. Do they have an unusual or particularly compelling sales pitch? Do they offer you something special?

Talk to some of their customers (be discreet). Find out what they like best about this competitor. Whatever you do, don't try to convince them you're better. In fact, don't even let them know that you are in the same business, or you won't get an honest answer.

Ask them what they think of the other companies around. See if your name even comes up. See what they say about your company, as well as every other competitor.

You don't have to be in retail to use this technique. Modify it to work in your type of business.

For example: If you are a distributor, call some of your biggest or toughest competitor's accounts on the phone. Act like a factory rep who is considering using this distributor, and find out what the account likes best about them. Ask the account about other distributors, and what they think of them.

If you are a manufacturer, talk to end users as well as people in every step of the distribution process. Find out why the retailers or reps push your products over someone else's, or why they don't.

It's amazing how "*out of touch*" most manufacturers are with the end users of their products. Sure, they do market research before they launch a product, and they do focus groups, but they rarely go into the trenches and talk to the people who are actually buying their products every day.

They rarely take the opportunity to watch customers shop and talk to them, right there on the spot, while they're actually making the buying decision.

How about professionals.

Here's where most professionals completely fail. (And they probably stand the most to gain from listening to their clients for a change).

Most professionals will be surprised when they find out what their clients really want.

And when they start filling these unfilled needs, they'll attract more clients than they'll be able to handle.

Many professionals seem to confuse being a competent practitioner who inspires confidence, with being *"uppity."*

They seem to feel that their time is more valuable than their patients' or clients'. Or they over-book appointments in case of cancellations which results in long waits when you show up for your appointment on time.

If professionals simply took the time to really get to know their clients and patients, find out what they really want... and started delivering it, the results would be staggering.

Every business will profit handsomely by simply finding out exactly what their customers want...

And then delivering it.

The operative phrase here is *"and then delivering it."*

Once you ascertain exactly what your customers want, you must decide if you can truly deliver it.

If you can, then do it. Don't just pay lip service to it, but really do it.

And do it better than anyone else.

But don't do it quietly, mind you.

If you don't blow your own horn, someone else will just use it for a spittoon!

Make some noise. Let the world know. Make sure you tell your customers that you asked them what they wanted, you listened to what they said, and you are delivering it.

Put up posters and signs in your store or office.

Put it in your advertising. Let all of the potential new customers out there know that you are prepared to deliver what they really want.

But remember, don't try to be all things to all people, because nobody will believe you. And if that happens, instead of being *everything* to *everyone*, you'll end up not being *anything* to *anyone*.

But we're getting ahead of ourselves, because this leads us into...

The Second Secret:

Every Business Needs An S.O.B.!

No, not some crotchety old man in accounting who throws a fit every time you spend a dime. And not some tough cigar-chewing manager who constantly complains about everything and everyone.

In fact, if you have anyone in your business like that, get rid of them. They're poison, and they're costing you a fortune!

This very important secret simply means that every business must have...

A Statement Of Benefit! (S.O.B)

This is a concise statement which tells everyone the single most compelling advantage they will gain by doing business with your company. It is what makes you unique and sets you apart from everyone else in the business. It tells the world what you do that puts you "*head and shoulders*" above all of your competitors.

Often, business owners reason: "*If I appear to offer every conceivable advantage that virtually anyone could want, I'll get all of the business.*"

What a mistake.

If you try to be all things to all people, you'll end up not being anything to anybody. You'll simply confuse the marketplace, and your potential customers will never know what you stand for or what you do best.

Remember, people want quick, painless, easy solutions to their problems, needs, and desires. If they're confused or unsure about what you really do, or what kind of goods you sell, or what level of service you provide, they won't bother to find out.

Develop a *Statement Of Benefit*.

In the last section, we talked about how to find out what your customers really want.

And once you find out what they want, you must determine which of those "*wants*" you can fill.

And lastly, you learned to make sure to tell them that you are the source to get those "*wants*" filled.

You do this with your S.O.B.

But don't come up with just anything. You need to give this some very serious consideration. Your S.O.B. should be *integrated into virtually everything you do,* so make sure that you pick one that fits your personality as well as one you can truly deliver.

You have to determine what really makes your company stand out from the crowd, and get this message out in all of your marketing efforts.

It could be that you carry three times the selection of any other dealer.

It could be that you only practice one specific specialty.

It could be that you are open seven days a week, 24 hours a day.

It could be that you stock only the top of the line highest quality goods.

It could be that your service department has more technicians so you can respond to a service call in two hours instead of two days.

Or, maybe you always have the lowest prices in town.

**Whatever it is, make certain that
your Statement Of Benefit comes
through in everything you do.**

Look at Federal Express.

Is there any doubt what their S.O.B. is? That's right, "*If it absolutely, positively has to be there..."*

How about Dominos Pizza?

That's right. *"30 minutes or free."*

You need to sit down and give this some serious thought. Develop your S.O.B. so that it truly reflects exactly who you are.

Keep it concise. Remember, it should be the single most important advantage the customer will gain by trading with you.

Don't be just another wandering generality.

It's critical to make sure that your S.O.B. really means something.

All too often, businesses adopt an S.O.B. that makes an empty, meaningless statement. Like *"The Lowest Prices In Town,"* or *"The Best Service Around."*

Don't do this.

It's totally unbelievable and unsubstantiated. Almost everyone says that they're the cheapest, or the best. Whatever your S.O.B. is, you've got to be specific and you've got to prove it.

For example, if you really have the lowest prices, and you decide that this kind of S.O.B. will allow you to command your market niche, present it in a factual, provable way rather than as an empty boast.

Find out how much cheaper you are than your competitors. Include the exact dollar or percentage difference in your S.O.B.

Or, you might present it as a minimum percentage of profit or markup.

Regardless of whether you use a percentage, or dollar figure, make certain of two things. First (and most importantly), make sure it's the truth. Secondly, make sure it's specific.

Be exact. Be precise. Be specific.

Platitudes and generalities are garbage. If your prices average 22.4% less than your competitor, use 22.4%. That's believable, because it appears to have been specifically measured. But, if you merely say, *"Over 20%,"* it sounds like an approximation, or worse yet, a guess. And that totally lacks credibility.

But, remember to center your S.O.B. around a significant and distinct benefit to the customer. Don't use your S.O.B. to merely brag or boast about how good you are. It won't work.

The customer doesn't care about your successes.

He doesn't care if you've got the newest equipment.

He doesn't care if you've won industry awards.

He doesn't care if you're the oldest, most established firm in town.

These things are all nice, and it's OK to be proud of them, but unless you present them in such a manner that they give your customer a direct and significant benefit, they're meaningless to him.

Customers will only react favorably to an S.O.B. that tells exactly what you'll do for them.

Some customers are more afraid of what a business will do *to* them rather than what the business will do *for* them. You've got to overcome that with great service and great products.

Use your S.O.B. to get that message across and then deliver on it, and you'll prosper. Ignore it, and you'll most likely fail.

Make this statement an integral part of every marketing effort. It should become your corporate soul... your image... your personality.

Remember, your S.O.B. is what triggers your name to come up in your customers' minds anytime they think of your product or service.

Once you begin to articulate this, you'll notice a big difference in your sales, because customers will know exactly what you'll do for them.

**Remember the old adage:
"A jack of all trades and master of none."**

If you want quality plumbing done, you want a master plumber, not just any handyman, don't you?

Well, your customers do too!

When you advertise, you should try to incorporate your S.O.B. into the headline of the ad.

Suppose that you find out that your customers want to be able to choose from a large selection.

You might run an ad that says something like:

**The average widget store carries 7 models of widgets.
A couple of them have 12 widgets...**

The Antin Widget Emporium always has 47 different widgets in all sizes and colors on display and in stock for immediate delivery!

Or...

**Why have to pick from 3 or 4 widgets
when Widget City always stocks 35
different widgets at discount prices?**

Or...

**Did you ever see a German widget?
How about an Italian designer widget?**

Well, World of Widgets now has a new selection of widgets from around the globe. Of course we also stock 38 American-made widgets (more than anyone else in town!)

What if you discover that more customers want faster in-home service?

You might base your S.O.B. on faster response times on service calls.

Try a headline like...

Wally's Widget Service has 12 expert factory-trained widget technicians on call 24 hours a day. We'll arrive at your door within 2 hours of your call or we'll fix your widget for free.

Or...

Most widget service people think widgets only break down between 9 and 5. We know better.

If your widget needs service, call Wally's Widget Repair. We'll be there within 2 hours whether you call us at 2:00 in the afternoon or 2:00 in the morning... or any time in between! If we're late, the repair is free.

Or...

The only way to get a widget repairman to your house faster than calling Wally's Widget Repair is to have him move into your guest room.

Suppose your customers tell you that they want only the highest quality, top of the line goods?

Try S.O.B. headlines like these...

**The Solid Gold Widget Company only
produced 1,000 of their 24 Carat model.**

Queen Elizabeth, George Bush, Sylvester Stallone, and Lee Iacocca each got one. That only leaves 996.

Here's how to get yours..

Or...

Quality furniture makers use hard wood frames... Comfy Couch uses only hand selected solid oak. Here's why...

Or...

Double The Manufacturer's Guarantee!

Exclusive Widgets is so picky in selecting the widgets that we stock, that we're even willing to Double The Manufacturer's Guarantee!

What if your customers want bargain-basement prices?

This is perhaps the easiest S.O.B. to promote.

Try things like...

Discount Widgets always has
$50 widgets for $25.

Or...

Discount Widgets will sell you any widget in stock for 11% less than any other store in town.
And we'll prove it.

Or...

Come to Discount Widgets and pick the widget you like, then use our phone to call around and find your best price.
We'll beat their price by 22%. Guaranteed!

Or...

Hi-Tech Widgets look and feel like $1,000 widgets, but you can still buy them for $200.

Or...

**We buy manufacturer's widget overstocks
at a fraction of the wholesale cost, and sell
them to you for pennies on the dollar.**

When you are thinking about what to base your S.O.B. on, make certain that it's something that will provide you with a large enough market to serve.

It certainly wouldn't do you any good to totally dominate a certain niche in your industry if there aren't enough customers that fall into that niche.

Don't forget that the market is always changing and evolving. A perfect market niche today might be dead in a year or two.

This doesn't mean necessarily that you shouldn't go for it anyway, just that you need to be aware of not only what's going on now in your industry, but where your industry is headed.

You can (and should) evolve your S.O.B. to move with the market. Don't allow yourself to become a dinosaur. You know what happened to them!

On the other hand, don't promiscuously change your S.O.B. to chase short-lived fads. That won't do you any good either.

Stay in touch with your customers, and you'll be able to recognize the difference between major market changes and the trivial crazes that soon blow over.

Let me give you an example.

One of our businesses was a small chain of electronics stores. We were lucky, because we jumped into that business at about the same time the first consumer video cassette recorders hit the market.

In the beginning, VCR's were so new and seemed so complex

that customers were almost afraid of them. We knew that the only way to sell a ton of VCR's was to help people understand and feel comfortable with them.

The first VCR's were very expensive, and they only appealed to people who could justify shelling out anywhere from $1,000 to $1,500.

These people were far more concerned about getting the proper guidance and instruction than they were about saving a few bucks.

Here's what we used for our S.O.B.

We'll teach you in plain English how to select the best VCR for you, and how to get the most out of it. Spend 30 minutes with our experts and your VCR will be as easy to use as your TV!

We sponsored clinics.

We gave lessons.

We set up our stores so that every VCR was hooked up to a TV and encouraged every customer to play with them.

After we helped our customers make their selection, we opened the box right in front of them, decided on the easiest way to hook it up to their TV and cable system, and even labeled the cables and hook-ups with tape so they didn't have to even open the owners manual.

**Sometimes, we even went to their homes
and hooked it up for them... FREE!**

We promised service and we delivered it in every way.

As you can guess, the business grew like a weed. Soon, we were by far the dominant VCR store in town.

Well, after a few years, the prices on VCR's plummeted. You could pick one up for a few hundred dollars. The market expanded to include thousands of people who had more modest spending habits.

These people still wanted selection and a certain degree of expertise and service, but they also wanted a fair price. VCR's were no longer some mysterious, complicated piece of equipment and almost anyone could afford one.

We had to change. Our S.O.B. no longer appealed to a large enough segment of the market to support our business.

Sure, there were still people who were mostly concerned with hand-holding and wanted a higher degree of personal service, but there were far more people who wanted to see it all, choose the one they wanted, and get it at a discount.

Our S.O.B. evolved to something like...

The 33 VCR's that we have on display represent every kind of VCR on the market. You can buy any one you want for 20% below the list price.

After a while, VCR's became more like a "commodity." Soon, almost all of the buyers were concerned only with the price. They didn't seem to care about service, or expertise, or anything else. All that mattered was the price.

Hey, we got into the electronics business because it was fun. The customers wanted and needed our help, and they were willing to pay a reasonable price for it.

They were as interested in everything about their new toy as we were, and we loved teaching them about it. *In fact, come to think about it, that's still what we're doing... teaching.*

Anyway, when the market turned to *"nothing matters but the price,"* the attitudes and personalities of the customers changed too. They couldn't care less about the details. They just wanted to save an extra $10.

This brings me to another very important point...

**When you decide on your S.O.B.,
make sure it's in sync with
your own personality and ability.**

We couldn't serve the *"nothing matters but the price,"* market... even if we wanted to.

To adopt that S.O.B. would have conflicted with everything we were and everything we liked about the business.

By the way, almost every industry evolves in some way. The market changes and the desires and wants of the customers change. But there is always a place for the full service, hand-holding S.O.B.

That market segment may not always be the biggest share of the market, but it almost always exists.

That's what happened to us. We had built a rather large business with 5 huge stores that brought with them a rather large overhead.

The market had finally evolved to a point where the number of customers who were still willing to pay for *any* level of service had dwindled. This small number of potential customers could no longer support our business.

Sure, we could have down-scaled our operation. We could have closed a few stores. But we felt that it was time to move on. We had other ideas, other markets, and other opportunities to explore.

Once you decide to go with your S.O.B., make certain that you do in fact live up to it... in every way. And make certain that you can *enjoy* living up to it.

If your S.O.B. is not really you, if it doesn't actually reflect your personality, you won't be any good at it no matter how hard you try.

If you just give lip service to it, your customers will see this and, believe me, the results won't be pretty.

If you make no promises and deliver nothing, it's bad, but if you do make promises and don't deliver on them, it's much, much worse.

Use a powerful S.O.B. to grab market share from established competitors... even in a mature industry!

Just because you happen to be in an industry that is already matured, don't ignore the many different and exciting S.O.B.'s that you could adopt to set you apart.

Suppose you were in the grocery business.

Grocery stores are about as mature an industry as you can find, but look at the different S.O.B.'s that are possible:

You could base your S.O.B. on the fact that you have the widest selection of fresh produce available anywhere. You could position yourself as the place to get any produce whether it's in season or not.

You could feature new and exotic produce. You could capitalize on the trend toward healthier eating. You could offer free recipes using some of this produce.

"We always stock 123 different varieties of farm fresh produce from around the world."

How about a S.O.B. based on gourmet foods?

"Global Foods carries 946 different hard-to-find ingredients for the 2,500 most popular gourmet recipes in the world."

You could set up several "*tasting booths*" around the store giving out free samples of various gourmet dishes. You could give every "*taster*" the printed recipe with the ingredients list. You might even include a discount coupon good for that day only.

Other grocers could base their S.O.B. on convenience.

"Why wait for 30 minutes to check out after 15 minutes of shopping? At Speedy Grocers, we promise that you'll never wait more than 3 minutes in line for a speedy cashier!"

They could post stock experts in every aisle who would not only tell customers where to find what they're looking for, but actually bring them right to the product.

How about a full service, more pleasurable shopping experience?

"Grocery shopping doesn't have to be a chore. Come to Grandma's Kitchen Cupboard and make your shopping a pleasure."

We've seen grocery stores like this. They have carpeted aisles, warm, cozy lighting, plenty of help, and all kinds of *"tasting stations."* You can nibble while you shop. They have a wide selection. They play nice music, and have a comfortable, homey decor that you hardly want to leave.

Another grocer could go with the warehouse pricing S.O.B.

"If you'll bring your own bags and boxes, we'll show you how to feed a family of 5 for less than most people spend feeding a family of 3!"

They have huge quantities of the most wanted and needed items. They go for the low price shopper who is looking for just the basics at the lowest possible price.

The point is that almost any kind of business could choose from several different S.O.B.'s that would make them extremely successful.

The key is to pick the right one for you, and then make certain that everyone in your organization knows (and lives up to) it.

Make certain that your S.O.B. does indeed become your company's heart and soul... from the top down.

If you promise fast service in your S.O.B., carry it through to everything you do. Make certain that your telephone is always answered on the first ring.

Make certain that you stock parts so you can complete the repairs quickly.

Make certain that you respond quickly in every aspect of your business; not just service calls, and not just to customers, but include vendors and suppliers in your new quick image.

Make it such that anytime anyone thinks of quick service, they automatically think of you!

The same thing is true no matter what you choose for your S.O.B.

Always make certain that your S.O.B. is evident and obvious in everything you do!

The Third Secret:

Why Talk To Just Anybody When You Could Be Selling Somebody?

Some time ago, we consulted with a dentist.

He had built a tremendous practice. In fact, he's one of the few professionals we've ever met who understands how to use marketing to build a professional practice.

Anyway, he recognized that most people view going to the dentist with the same enthusiasm as undergoing an I.R.S. audit.

He knew that most people still consider dental work a painful ordeal.

But he also knew that he could perform almost any dental procedure virtually painlessly on almost any patient.

So he wrote a newspaper ad with the following headline...

We Cater To Cowards!

He went on to tell the reader that dental health is so important to a person's overall health and quality of life, that he felt it was a shame that so many people neglect their dental needs because of the perception that dental care has to hurt.

He continued by telling them how he had developed his own special methods of removing all of the pain from his dental procedures.

He told them about the many special seminars and conferences he had attended to keep up on all of the state of the art techniques to eliminate the pain.

And so on and so forth.

Frankly, it was a pretty good ad. But it wasn't a great ad.

Take another look at his headline...
"We Cater To Cowards"

Who is he "*talking*" to?

Is it obvious with just a glance?

Or, do you have to read the entire ad to know what it's talking about?

Does the headline specifically call out to his best prospect?

Or... Does it "*talk*" to just anybody out there?

Suppose you happened to be suffering from a tooth ache, and you really weren't looking forward to going to a dentist. You're sitting at your kitchen table glancing through the paper. Would that headline absolutely force you to read the ad?

Maybe. Maybe not.

That's exactly where the problem lies.

Many businesses use humorous, clever, or catchy headlines to try to attract everyone's attention. They create advertising for the masses.

This is a very costly mistake, because...

The masses don't buy your products
and services, individuals do!

And not just any individual, either... only the individuals who want what you are selling.

Sure, "*We cater to cowards*" is cute, and if you already knew what the ad was talking about it might mean something, but it's far too general for a headline.

It really doesn't reach out and grab his best prospect.

It doesn't tell the reader that this ad is addressed specifically to him and that he should read it right now to learn how to solve his problem.

If you saw that headline, you might think it was an ad for karate lessons, or personal body guards, or hand gun shooting lessons, or assertiveness training, or any other product or service that "*caters to cowards.*"

When you create any piece of advertising, remember to keep your focus on who you want to read the ad *(which should only be those people most likely to act on your offe*r).

*I'm two weeks behind schedule because my stone tools keep
breaking. Why can't someone make tools that last longer.*

The first place that this focus becomes evident is in the headline.

Every ad needs a headline!
The headline is actually an ad for the ad.

Most people read the paper by scanning the headlines, and if a particular headline catches their eye and promises information that they want, they'll start to read the story below it.

But if the story doesn't immediately begin to deliver what is promised in the headline, the reader will quickly move on to something else.

Sound familiar?

There are a few people who actually read the paper cover to cover, but they certainly don't read every word of every ad.

Anyway, the same concept is true with advertising (except that the readers have even less patience with ads). The readers merely glance at the headlines. If a particular headline grabs their attention, they may begin to read the rest of the ad.

But if the ad doesn't immediately start to deliver what the headline promises... they'll move on.

People will always read what interests them (even ads), but they will not allow you to bore them in print.

Cute, funny headlines may attract more curiosity seekers, but many of your best prospects might not get the joke. They might not make the connection between the headline and the product or service that they would be willing to buy, and therefore not read the ad.

And as soon as the curiosity seekers realize they don't want what you're selling, they'll simply move on to something else.

The end result is that you've missed out on the opportunity to sell a great many of your best prospects, and instead, spent a fortune just to entertain a bunch of curiosity seekers.

On the other hand, very focused headlines that promise a distinct benefit or specific piece of news that is of interest to your best prospect will attract virtually all of those people who are most likely to become your customers. And it doesn't matter if non-prospects read it or not.

Let's look at some actual examples that we pulled out of our morning paper.

Here's the first one...

"Company's coming and you're not home"

Have you got a clue as to what they're selling?

Maybe it's an ad for a new fast food pickup service, or a new telephone answering machine. Or, maybe you guessed that it's for outdoor lighting.

Well, you're getting warm. It's actually an ad for a home security company.

They're advertising a monitored home alarm system that costs $195 for installation plus $19.95 per month.

A lot of people who are, in fact, concerned about the security of their homes might not get the joke, and fail to read the ad.

Here's a headline that we might have tried.

1 out of 14 homes in our city will be burglarized in 1992.

We'll carefully watch over your
home and family for only 67 cents a day.

Here's another one...

"The Home Team Advantage"

What is this about?

Could it be for the hometown sports team, or the local chamber of commerce?

In fact, it could be for any local business.

But in this case, the ad is for a real estate office.

They were trying to attract people who would allow them to list their homes for sale.

Here's a better one...

If You Want To Sell Your Home

Here's eleven important ways to get more money out of your home, and sell it in half the time.

Here's one more example. The headline said...

"You'll Like The Sound Of This!"

Is it for a new stereo? A concert? Or maybe a super-quiet new luxury car?

This headline is really on an ad for a new hearing aid.

They were offering a new fit-in-the-ear hearing aid that reduces background noise automatically.

Here's a possible headline that might work better...

Amazing new hearing aid helps you hear what you want to hear and cuts annoying background noise by a whopping 93%!

Now that you've seen some actual examples, lets's get back to our dentist friend.

We asked him specifically who he was trying to reach with this ad.

He said he wanted to reach anyone who was neglecting their dental care because they dread going to the dentist, as well as those people who don't neglect their dental care, but would prefer to go to a painless dentist.

We agreed that his obvious S.O.B. (remember, that's *"Statement Of Benefit"*) is...

We practice painless dentistry.

Now, that would be a pretty good headline by itself, wouldn't it? It does tell the reader what the ad is about, doesn't it?

We wanted something even more specific. We want to home in on exactly the people we want to reach.

We want the ad to call out to them as if it had their name on it. We want the headline to reach out, grab the prospect by the hand, drag his attention over to the ad, and literally force him to read it.

Here's the headline that we told him to use (actually it consists of a subhead above the headline and a subhead below the headline) ....

Are you one of the millions of people who puts off going to the dentist because it hurts?

Completely Painless Dentistry Is Now A Reality!

If you'd like to receive quality, professional dental care with absolutely no pain, you simply must read this important announcement...

Do you see how it literally calls out specifically to his best prospect?

Is there any way that someone who has a tooth ache, or someone who knows they've been putting off going to the dentist would not be interested in the information following a headline like this?

Of course not!

Do you see how the subhead below the headline tells that best prospect exactly what to do next to gain the benefit he seeks?

Do you see how the ad is already selling to that specific individual?

Do you see how we left absolutely no doubt as to who we're talking to and what we we're talking about?

Notice how, rather than talking to anybody, this ad is selling to somebody, and that somebody is our very best prospect!

The rest of the ad told the prospect all about the benefits he or she will experience just by becoming one of this particular dentists's very special patients.

Continue to sell to that specific prospect.

Once you get the prospect hooked by specifically talking to him in the headline, continue talking specifically to him throughout the rest of the ad.

Don't confuse the issue by including facts, features, or other information that will not appeal specifically to this particular prospect.

If you also want to attract a prospect with a different need or want, do it in another ad.

Look at it this way...

Your advertising is read by one person at a time, it should talk to one person at a time! No, make that SELL to one person at a time!

We've been using a newspaper ad as the example here, but of course, the same holds true for any print advertising, or TV advertising, or radio advertising, or any other advertising.

Sometimes the most effective sales message is not the most "politically correct" message.

You know, sometimes the things that will appeal to one person will offend another.

Sometimes the perfect sales message that would cause one person to literally start drooling over your product or service might be completely revolting to someone else.

Well, unless you're a politician running for re-election, forget what's politically correct...

Forget trying to please everybody...

Forget worrying about people who aren't likely to do business with you anyway, and concentrate instead on selling the ones who will.

Now, don't get me wrong. I'm not suggesting you go out of your way to offend people in your advertising. That's ridiculous, because those people might someday become legitimate prospects.

But, I am suggesting that you do not water down your sales message to your prospects in order to be more palatable to someone who is not your prospect.

In fact, to give you the best, most graphic, true life example of this concept puts us in an awkward situation.

You see, this example is quite sexist. You may find it slightly offensive.

On the other hand, it really is the perfect example to hammer home a very important point, so we decided to risk it.

Several years ago, a very good friend of ours, Gary Halbert, (one of the best marketing and advertising minds on the planet) broke off a long term relationship with his "*significant other.*"

Well, after spending every single evening and weekend alone for a few weeks, he started dating again... unsuccessfully.

None of the women he dated were "*the perfect woman*" for him.

He knew that there had to be a better way, so he devised a plan.

First, he sat down and thoroughly and honestly evaluated what he had to offer "*the perfect woman.*"

Then, he determined exactly what he was looking for in "*the perfect woman.*"

He decided that he wanted a "hot, sexy woman with a good sense of humor."

Of course, he wanted some other things too, but regardless of the other qualifications, his "*perfect woman*" had to be hot, sexy, and have a good sense of humor.

Guess what he did next.

He wrote an ad!

Not your typical "*personals*" ad, mind you...

He wrote and placed a full page ad in one of the country's largest newspapers!

Here's the headline that he used...

Are you more than just another pretty face?

Generous Creative Businessman Wants to Find a Hot, Sexy Woman With a Good Sense of Humor

Notice how he is only talking to his perfect prospect?

Well, the rest of the ad talked specifically to the "*hot, sexy women*" that he felt would read it. He focused on things that he hoped would appeal to a hot sexy woman.

He told her about how he works out to keep in shape.

He told her about the things he likes to do.

He told her how he likes to buy little presents for the woman in his life.

He told her that he likes to take little mini-vacations or long weekends to Hawaii, and the Bahamas, and Acapulco with his lover.

But he also mentioned things that were important to him...

He told her that he wants someone "*that will take my breath away when I see her in a string bikini!*"

And he told her that... "*I like women who take care of themselves. If you have a slender, healthy body, a reasonably slim waist, a very pretty face and a good sense of humor then, quite frankly, you sound like heaven to me!*"

Think about it. If you were a woman who worked hard to stay in shape, wouldn't you want to be with a man who appreciated it?

And if you worked hard to stay in shape, wouldn't you want a man who kept himself in great shape, also?

Don't you think an attractive woman (or anyone else, for that matter) likes to be treated well... likes to receive little presents... likes to go on little vacations... and is generally proud of being attractive?

Well, as you can imagine, my friend got several letters from women who thought his ad was sexist.

And, according to him, there were a lot of "unattractive humorless women who didn't like his ad"

"But, you should have seen the hundreds of gorgeous, intelligent, hot sexy women who did like it."

He was virtually flooded with replies from these "*perfect women*".

When we asked him why he wrote an ad which would obviously offend some of the people who would see it, he looked us right straight in the eye and said...

"In any selling situation, you should always concentrate more on selling the 'FOXES' and don't worry about offending the 'DOGS'!"

We hope you found the example more instructional than offensive, but in case we guessed wrong, we'd like to ask you to do us one little favor.

If you think that we should have not used this example, please write to us at the address in the back of the book and tell us.

Of course, if you agree with our decision to use this example, please write and tell us that also.

We'll read every comment, and if the majority of our readers think we shouldn't use it, we'll take it out of future editions of the book.

And if our readers think that it is a worthwhile example, we'll keep it in the book.

In fact, while we're on the subject, please write us with any comments you may have. Whether you liked or loathed this book, we'd like to hear from you. But we'd really like to hear how you were able to use the secrets to become even more successful.

We really do care.

Why are we willing to base our future decisions on your wishes? Well, remember secret number one?

We don't want to answer our own questions.

But for now, let's turn our attention to secret number four...

The Fourth Secret:

Don't Let Your Advertising
Be All Show And No Go!

This "*secret*" should really be applied to everything you do. Not just your advertising.

Remember when we talked about the changing attitudes and mind-set of the American people?

Well, they want "*the real thing*." They don't want a cheap imitation, they don't want just a fancy cover. They want substance. They want the "*meat*."

Here's a perfect example that happened to us just a few days ago...

We are both boxing fans, and the other day we went down to the arena to watch the fights.

Now, these were professional fights, although certainly not championship quality. In fact, the boxers were all local boys just starting out. They were trying to build a name (and record) for themselves.

Anyway, they introduced the first fighter and he got into the ring and did a little bit of stretching, and shadow boxing just to loosen up.

He looked like an old style fighter wearing plain black boxing trunks with a white stripe. In fact, he wouldn't have looked out of place in one of those old "*Friday Night At The Fights*" shows.

Next, his opponent got into the ring. You should have seen this guy. He was wearing white sequined bikini briefs and his boxing shoes had more tassels hanging from them than you'd see in an acre of corn. He even had his name cut into his hair.

My goodness. Anyone who dressed like that had better be a good fighter!

Everyone figured that this would be a great fight. This flashy young boxer was really playing to the crowd. He danced around the ring, shadow boxing, and he even did a couple of back flips.

He really whipped the crowd into a frenzy. We were all on our feet in expectation of a great fight.

Well, the bell sounded, and the fight began. The guy in the black trunks came out of his corner and walked to the center of the ring. He had a determined look in his eyes. He looked ready for action.

At the same time, the flashy kid danced out of his corner, and started showing off. He started dancing around the other fighter (well out of range of being hit) and threw some punches into thin air.

I guess he was trying to intimidate the other guy, but it didn't seem to be working.

The funny part is that he never moved in close enough to hit the other guy, even if he'd had a *"ten foot pole."* He just danced around, throwing punches into thin air as if he were still shadow boxing.

But the crowd had paid to see a fight, and frankly, we were getting impatient.

Towards the end of the first round, he was still playing around, paying more attention to the crowd than to his opponent.

Finally, with only about 15 seconds left in the round, the guy in the black trunks got close enough to land a punch. He nailed the *"showboat"* with a solid left hook.

Well, the showboating stopped in a hurry. The kid's legs turned to jello and he sank to the canvas.

That was it. The fight was over.
The entire fight consisted of exactly one punch.

That "*showboat*" sure had all of the style. He had all of the moves. He was flashy and well decorated. In fact, he was a lot of things...

But he certainly wasn't much of a boxer! He pretended to be a boxer. But he didn't deliver.

He was "all show and no go!"

And that's exactly the same problem that plagues most of the advertising we see in business today.

Unless you have an almost limitless amount of money which you can pour down a "*black hole,*" this is going to be a very important chapter to you, so pay close attention.

Almost all advertising falls into one of two types...

Image Advertising (The Show)
Or...
Direct Response Advertising (The Go)

Guess which type we recommend.

We are writing this chapter under the assumption that you believe (as we do) that the only reason a business would advertise is to get more customers, and sell more products and services.

With that in mind, let's look at these two types of advertising.

First, consider image advertising (some people call this institutional advertising, but we'll use the term "*image,*" because it's more descriptive of what it really is).

This is frequently the kind of advertising that you see from banks, insurance companies, large manufacturers, and in fact, most big "*corporate*" type businesses (or those wishing to appear as such).

*Well, what did you expect from the "**Biggest Bank**"?*

This kind of advertising usually tries to convey a certain *"image"* about the company paying for the ad.

It attempts to tell the prospect how great the company is.

It attempts to make the prospect believe that this company is more trustworthy, honest, or kinder than their competitors.

It attempts to give the company a look of professionalism or strength.

It attempts to make the prospects feel good about the company.

It attempts to make the prospects feel that this is the kind of company that they'd like to do business with.

The focus of most image advertising seems to be *"me, me, me."* The advertiser is suggesting that the prospect buy from *"me"* without ever telling the prospect exactly what's in it for *"him."*

It's almost as if the only sales message in image ads is... *"Buy from me because I'm telling you that I'm a great company."* or, *"Buy from me because I can afford to pay for this ad."* or, *"Buy from me because I'm greedy and I want your business."*

Let's look at what image advertising doesn't do.

It doesn't tell the prospect about any distinct advantage or benefit that he'll gain by doing business with the company in the ad.

It doesn't make a complete or compelling case for any particular product or service.

It doesn't make a specific offer.

It doesn't tell the prospect to take any specific action.

But the biggest problem with image advertising is that it doesn't provide a way for the company paying for the ad to determine what (if any) results that the ad is generating for them.

In short, image advertising concentrates more on cultivating customer attitudes than stimulating customer action!

At its best, I mean if you look at it in its most generous light, image advertising *may* produce some delayed sales.

In other words, it's possible, that if you spend enough money to keep your image in front of the prospect's face, eventually, when he's ready to buy, he *"may"* remember your name and consider your product or service. But don't count on it.

Generally speaking, image advertising is a worthless and wasteful expenditure of a company's assets.

Not only does image advertising fail to provide a tangible return on investment, it prevents the company from using those same resources in a manner that would.

So, why do so many large corporations use image advertising?

One reason could be that the people who own these companies

(the stockholders) and the people who run them and make the decisions (the management) have different goals.

The management wants to keep their jobs, and the stockholders want to make money on their investments.

And although the stockholders really do want to see the company make money, they aren't marketing experts. They like to see sharp, glitzy, image-building campaigns. It makes them feel good. It's great for the ego to point to them and say "*I own part of that company.*"

If the management keeps the stockholders happy, they get to keep their jobs. Of course, if the company loses money, they sometimes get bounced, but the new management does essentially the same thing.

Of course not all image advertising is a waste. If the company develops a strong, trustworthy image, it could help generate interest in their stock. But frankly, that job should be accomplished by good public relations and publicity rather than advertising.

When a big corporation loses money, they always pin the blame on runaway expenses, or too poor a work force, or a bad economy.

But the real reason is usually that they just failed to convince a sufficient number of customers to buy enough of their products or services.

Maybe they should take a look at their advertising?

By the way, it seems like these companies always use the "*top advertising agencies*" in the world.

How does an agency get to the top?

Well, the advertising industry gives itself awards for the best ad campaigns. They're called *Clio's*. The agency that gets the most *Clio's*, seems to get the most big clients.

But that brings up a major problem. Since image advertising, by its very nature, does not provide any tangible way of tracking the results (if any) that it generates, these awards are given out based solely on creativity and originality.

The question of whether or not the campaign made any money for the client never enters the decision.

How ridiculous!

Many of the *"creatives"* behind these *"winning"* advertising campaigns are probably frustrated artists who use the advertising medium merely to showcase their artistic talents.

Well, the only "art" that our clients want to see is "art" that has pictures of dead presidents... in the color green!

But the advertising agencies like their system. This way, they can't be held accountable for hard-core results. They merely have to provide creativity and entertainment.

There's another thing about the system that the agencies like. They get paid a percentage of the amount of money that they can convince a client to spend on TV time, radio time, newspaper ads, magazine ads, billboards, and everything else.

But wait a minute, you say...

Isn't the sole purpose of advertising to get more customers, and sell more products and services?

It sure is, so hold that thought as we look at...

Direct Response Advertising.

Direct Response Advertising is very easy to understand. Just look at its name. This is advertising that is designed to elicit an immediate, predictable, measurable response from the prospect.

A direct response ad doesn't waste any time or space making empty boasts about the company running the ad. Instead, it concentrates on making a sale.

First, it makes a specific offer to the prospect.

Then it makes a complete and compelling case for the product or service being offered.

Then it proves to the prospect that the product or service advertised will solve some problem in the prospect's life or provide some valuable benefit to him.

It provides hard, specific numbers, facts, and statistics, as well as testimonials from other customers or respected people to validate their claims.

Then it tells the prospect the reason why this offer is so good and why the company is able to make such an attractive offer.

It tells the prospect *exactly* what to do next to gain these remarkable benefits or solutions.

Then it creates urgency by telling the prospect that he must act now in order to gain these important benefits, and why this offer is so limited, either by time, or by the quantity available of what's being offered.

And finally, it contains some way for the business owner to track exactly what sales or customers were generated by that particular ad.

"Hey, wait a minute," you say...

This sounds like a sales pitch!

Give yourself a "*gold star,*" because you're exactly right.

There's nothing mysterious or magical about advertising. It's really not a "*voodoo*" science.

Good advertising is just salesmanship.

It's simply salesmanship MULTIPLIED!

Instead of only talking to one prospect at a time, like your live salespeople do, your advertising can sell to *thousands* of people at the same time.

The moment you start to look at, and judge, your advertising in the same way you judge your salespeople, you'll be way ahead of the crowd.

Would you continue to pay a salesperson who simply doesn't make any sales, or not enough sales to pay for his keep? Of course not.

Well don't do that with your advertising, either.

Remember... Your advertising is just another salesperson.

You should be ruthlessly demanding of both. A mediocre salesperson will only affect a small part of your business, but mediocre (or image) advertising will affect *all* of your business!

The attributes that make the difference between a "*world class*" salesperson and a mediocre one are the same attributes that make your advertising either "*world class*" or mediocre.

Look at your best salesperson (or any extremely successful salesperson)...

Does that salesperson simply say to a prospect... "*Buy my goods because they're the best*" and nothing more?

Of course not. Don't let your advertising do it either.

Does this "*world class*" salesperson deliver fancy, colorful speeches, or does he present a complete and compelling case for the product in plain, easy to understand language?

When you're writing an ad, ask yourself... *"Would a "world class" salesperson say that?"*

If the answer is "no," then you probably shouldn't put it in your advertising.

But you *should* put in everything and anything that a "*world class*" salesperson would say to convince the prospect to buy. (Of course, this is based on an honest and ethical salesperson who *tells the truth*.)

Don't think, for a moment, that this will make your ads too long.

Some of the "*experts*" say that you must keep your copy (this is the words in your ad) short. They say that people won't read a long ad.

They say that people have very short attention spans, that long ads are boring, and the prospect won't read them.

Our answer to these people is simply...

"Hogwash!", "In a pig's eye!", And ### *"That's ridiculous!"*

They fall into the old cliche about having "*just enough knowledge to be dangerous.*" They're on the right track, but they're getting off at the wrong station.

You see, they are taking a very important rule about advertising and totally misapplying it.

That rule is:

People will not let you bore them in print!

And it's absolutely true.

Do you remember the last section, "*Why Talk To Just Anybody When You Could Be Selling Somebody*"?

We said that...

"People will always read what interests them (even ads), but they will not allow you to bore them in print."

Those people who say you must keep your ads short, because prospects won't read a long ad, are missing the most important point.

That is, that people *will* read what interests them!

Put it this way. If someone is not interested in your product or service, they're probably not going to read your ad whether it is long *or* short.

And even if they did, they wouldn't act on it, so it doesn't matter anyway.

But, if they *are* interested in your product or service, they're going to want to know *everything* there is to know about it.

Here's where your ads are just like your salespeople. They've got to tell the prospect every reason why *that* prospect should purchase your goods and services.

Could you imagine going up to your best salesperson and saying:

"You know, Frank, people don't want to be bored, so from now on, you can only say 25 words to a prospect when you are trying to sell them."

That's silly, isn't it?

Well, anyone who tells you to use only short copy in your ads is basically telling you the same thing.

Don't listen to them.

But don't go overboard in the other direction, either. Don't pad your ads with empty, meaningless garbage just to create the illusion of *"telling all."*

Only put into your ads those things that will help motivate a prospect to buy. Nothing else.

Remember the *"acid test."* If a salesperson would think it's important to say, say it. If not, don't.

Now that you're thinking about your ads as salespeople, let's go to the next *"secret"* and look at the types of things that you *should* say in your ads...

The Value Of A Good Education!

We're not talking about academics, mind you, but the fact that you have to educate your customers.

You have to educate them about your industry...

You have to educate them about your company...

You have to educate them about your products and services...

You have to educate them about your offers...

And you have to educate them about all of the wonderful things that you do for them.

Educating your prospects and customers is the most powerful weapon in your marketing arsenal.

In this chapter we're going to talk about three distinct ways you should educate your customers and potential customers. Each of these is tailored to a specific purpose.

Educating 101 -- A Bigger Piece Of The Pie.

This is when you educate prospects about the advantages of your product or service over other, competing products or services. The basic goal here is to increase your market share.

Educating 202 -- A Bigger Pie.

This is where you use educating to actually enlarge the market. The goal here is to teach people who are not yet even in the market for your products or services about the reasons why they should be. When you do it right, most of the new market you create will automatically become yours.

Educating 303 -- Pie Protection.

This is often the most overlooked way to educate your customers. If neglected, your existing customers could fall prey to a competitor's Educating 101. In other words, you have to continue communicating with, and educating, your customers on an ongoing basis if you want to keep them as customers. If you fail in this kind of educating, one of your competitors could easily take them away from you.

Let's start with Educating 101.

After reading the last *"secret,"* you now know that you should use only direct response advertising, and that good direct response advertising is in reality just salesmanship multiplied.

And good salesmanship is primarily a process of educating your prospects into becoming customers.

You must teach them all about your product, your company, and your industry. When you do it properly, they usually decide to buy (assuming they were qualified prospects in the first place).

Well, you should do the same thing in your advertising.

For example, suppose you manufacture a particularly good quality widget. And your widget sells for a little more than the average widget, but since it's the best widget available anywhere, it's worth it.

Perhaps your widget uses half inch steel instead of the industry standard quarter inch...

Perhaps the bearings in your widget are machined to within .0001 inch instead of the industry standard .001 inch...

Perhaps your widget uses gold-plated electrical connections instead of the industry standard copper connections...

Perhaps your widget comes with a one year guarantee instead of the industry standard 90 days...

Naturally, you put these extras into your widget because they each provide a tangible benefit to the consumer.

They might make your widget last longer, or perform better under extreme conditions, or perform more consistently.

Whatever the reason and whatever the associated benefit, you can bet that a "*world class*" salesperson makes sure to educate the prospect as to the importance and advantages of these features.

Well, you should do that
in your advertising, too!

Remember, your advertising is just another salesperson. It "*talks*" to hundreds or thousands of people at the same time, but it needs to present the same features and benefits that a salesperson does.

Don't take it for granted that the prospects know about your product or service. They don't!

If you use half inch steel instead of quarter inch, your ads should tell them.

If you use only the very best components in your manufacturing process, your ads should tell them.

If you search the world for the most unique or valuable goods, your ads should tell them.

In short, your ads should tell them everything you do for them.

Of course, sometimes your product or service may not be radically different than your competitors. Perhaps you're in an industry that is quite mature and stable, and everyone does things more or less the same way.

If that's the case, and you can't think of anything that's remarkably different about your specific product or service, look at your industry in general.

Chances are that if everyone does things the same way, there's a good reason for it. And there's an equally good chance that nobody ever explained it to the consumers.

Here's where you could use a very, very powerful educating/marketing technique.

It's called *"preemptive"* advertising.

Just as a *"preemptive"* strike is when you strike first in such a way as to prevent your opponent from striking back, *"preemptive"* advertising is when you advertise something in such a way as to make it difficult (or impossible) for your competitors to strike back.

Probably the best way to explain this technique is to relate a story told by the late, great Claude C. Hopkins (arguably the father of modern advertising).

Not too long after the turn of the century, Schlitz Beer, the fifth largest seller of beer in the country, hired Claude Hopkins to help them increase their market share.

At that time, the rage in beers was purity. All of the big brewers were blasting the word *"Pure"* in their advertising. In fact, they would often spend a fortune to take out huge, double-page ads so they could write the word *"Pure"* in even bigger letters than the competition.

They were on the right track, because the beer drinkers of the country were quite concerned about the purity of their beer. So the brewers were addressing a valid and important *"want"* of their potential customers.

Well, Hopkins knew that empty claims of *"purity,"* combined with the fact that everyone was boasting about their *"purity,"* weren't going to make much of an impression on too many people.

He knew that he had to tell people more, that he had to educate them.

Hopkins wasn't an expert on beer, so he went on a tour of the Schlitz brewery. What an eye-opener!

He saw these massive plate glass rooms where beer was dripping down over cooling pipes. When he asked the reason for these special rooms, he was told that these rooms were filled with carefully filtered air so that the beer would remain completely pure as it cooled.

He saw several huge filters that contained white-wood pulp, and was told that although this special pulp was quite expensive, it provided a much better filtering process than anything else available.

He saw men carefully clean every pump and pipe not once, but twice each day to eliminate the chance of any contamination getting into the beer.

He saw how every beer bottle was cleaned and sterilized not once or twice, but four separate times by special steam cleaning machinery before it was filled with beer.

The Schlitz brewery was located right on Lake Michigan. The lake wasn't the least bit polluted at the time, and could have easily and inexpensively provided them with more clean water than they would ever need. But that wasn't good enough for Schlitz.

The brewers showed Hopkins the special artesian well that they had dug (4,000 feet deep) to provide the purest, cleanest possible water.

Then they took him to the laboratory and showed him the original mother yeast cell. They explained that this yeast cell was the product of over 1,200 separate experiments designed to bring out the utmost in flavor.

Every bit of the yeast that is ever used in brewing Schlitz Beer was developed from that original mother cell.

When he got back to the Schlitz office, he was totally amazed.

He couldn't understand why Schlitz didn't tell the beer buying public about all of the incredible steps that they go through to make sure that their beer is so good.

With such a powerful story to tell, he couldn't understand why they merely tried to "*scream*" the word "*Pure*" louder in their advertising than the other brewers.

He suggested that they base their entire ad campaign on teaching beer drinkers about the specific techniques and processes that Schlitz Beer used to virtually guarantee pure, great tasting beer.

The Schlitz people thought he was nuts. They told him that the processes they use are the same processes that any other brewer uses. They said that this was simply the way it was done and that no one can make good beer any other way.

Hopkins pointed out how amazed anyone who had gone through their brewery (including himself) was at the process, and that no other brewer had ever told the story before. He said that when beer drinkers read about those processes in the Schlitz ads, they would also be amazed, and they would want to taste the results of such diligent brewing.

They gave the go ahead, and Hopkins created the ads. He featured those great glass rooms with the filtered air, and he told the complete story.

The result... Purity now had a meaning. They gave the beer drinkers the reasons why their beer was pure, and the beer drinkers responded -- in droves.

Schlitz was suddenly catapulted from fifth place to neck and neck for first, within just a few months. All because they had educated their customers.

Any brewer could have told the same story, but none of them did. They couldn't see any advantage to be gained by telling people something so common to their industry.

They missed the powerful "*Common Sense*" solution that was right under their noses!

Of course, after Schlitz "*broke the story,*" any other brewer could have told the same story, because they did the same things. But Schlitz had "*preempted*" them. If the other brewers merely copied the story, the public would have just figured that they were "*me too's,*" and would have still probably opted for Schlitz.

But teaching your prospects the "*nuts and bolts*" about your product or service is only one area in which you must educate them. And you can't really do that until they at least acknowledge (to themselves, anyway) that they are indeed thinking of buying what you're selling.

In other words, what good would it do for you to teach me all about your widget and how your widget is superior to all other widgets, if I don't even think that I need a widget?

This brings us to Educating 202.

Sometimes, you need to educate a *"suspect"* into becoming a prospect. (By *"suspect,"* we are referring to anyone who should be a prospect for your product or service, but doesn't know it yet.)

You've heard the old adage that if you give a man a fish, you'll feed him for a day, but if you teach him to fish, you'll feed him for life?

Let's put a little twist on it.

Teach him to fish and then
sell him a bunch of fishing gear.

You'd be amazed at how many good quality "prospects-to-be" *(suspects)* are out there just waiting for you to teach them to be prospects.

Let's look at a marketing problem that another client brought to us, and how the simple technique of educating *"suspects"* really paid off for him.

This guy is a dentist. No, not the one with the *"We Cater To Cowards"* ad. This dentist specializes in pediatric (children's) dental care. He's a pediadontist.

Anyway, he is a great dentist, his patients (and their parents) absolutely love him, and he is one of just a few pediadontists in town.

You would think that his practice would be bursting at the seams.

But he had a problem.

Most parents of very young children don't even know what a

pediadontist is, let alone that they should bring their children to see one.

Many of these parents wait until their children have a full set of teeth before they ever bring them to a dentist, and then, they just bring them to their own regular dentist.

Our pediadontist explained that a person's dental health for their entire life can be significantly enhanced by getting an early start on regular dental care.

He taught us about the many dental problems (some minor and some not so minor) that can be corrected or even avoided by early detection and treatment.

He gave us some simple tips and techniques that parents could use to make teething much, much easier on them as well as their children, and even mentioned that he was always willing to perform the first exam on a new pediatric patient at no charge.

His enthusiasm for his work and his love of the kids came through in everything he did.

You should see his offices and waiting room... If you did, you'd understand why his young patients love going to see him. I saw some kids there who were having so much fun that they didn't want to leave!

Well, his marketing problem was not convincing parents to bring their children to him *instead* of some other pediatric dentist. He was already doing much of the pediatric dental care in town.

Actually, he had a two-part marketing problem.

First, he had to teach parents that they should take their children to *any* dentist at an earlier age.

And secondly, he had to teach them that as long as they were going to take their very young child to a dentist, they should choose a dentist who specializes in pediatric dentistry, such as himself.

**We solved both parts of this marketing
problem with a series of simple letters.**

First, we had our dentist friend start collecting all of the new birth announcements in his trade area, and enter the date of birth, names, and addresses of both the parents and babies into his computer.

We knew from talking to him that a child should really have his first dental exam at about six months of age, so we told him to send a letter to the parents when the child was five months old.

Remember, most of these parents are not yet in the market for a pediadontist, and many of them don't even know what a pediadontist is, so this is not going to be a "*hard core*" sales letter.

This first effort should be more of a nurturing, caring, educational letter to the parents.

It went something like this...

Dear Mr. and Mrs. Smith,

By now you've probably received a ton of congratulations on the birth of your son (or daughter), and even though your child was born five months ago, let me add my congratulations to the list.

You might think that it's a little odd that I waited so long to write, but since what I have to tell you is quite important, I decided to wait until you had a chance to get used to having your new baby and catch up on some badly needed rest.

I remember when my kids were born, and it seemed that it took a while before I regained the luxury of sleeping through the night without being awakened by a crying baby.

By now, your child is probably teething, and may be having a hard time of it. So, I thought that you might like to know a few of the "*secrets*" I've found to help your child through this difficult time (as well as help mommy and daddy get a decent night's sleep).

By the way, my name is Dr. Richard Jones, and I'm a pediadontist.

That simply means that I am a dentist who specializes in treating children.

When your child starts acting irritably, carefully look and feel around his gums. If you feel a tooth starting to push through, you can probably bet that it's the source of the discomfort.

Try this...

[Then the letter went on to explain a few different things that the parent can try to stop the pain]

I hope this helps, but if it doesn't, feel free to give my office a call, and we'll try to help you as much as we can over the phone.

By the way, did you know that your baby should really have his first dental exam at around six months of age?

It's true.

This is actually quite important to your child's future dental health, and can frequently head off some of the common dental problems that older kids have down the road.

[He explained some of those problems]

You know, Mr. and Mrs. Smith, I feel so strongly about this first dental exam, that I'd like to buy this exam for you with my compliments.

Why don't you call my office this week and schedule an appointment to bring your child in to see me. My number is 123-1234. I'll perform this very important initial exam, and give you a complimentary copy of a special report that I've written on pediatric dental care.

Don't worry, this report is not written for doctors or scientists, it's written specifically for parents, and will certainly save you a bunch of time, effort, and worry as your child develops both his baby teeth and his adult set.

By the way, don't be too surprised when you see my office, it's designed specifically for my most important visitors -- your children.

Frankly, I've been told that it looks more like a "*Sesame Street*" playground than a doctor's office, and my patients do seem to hate to leave, but I feel that it's important that your child should learn to look forward to good dental health care rather than grow up dreading the dentist.

Anyway, I hope the "*teething tips*" help, and I look forward to seeing you soon.

Warmly,

Dr. Richard Jones

P.S. The complete exam and the report are my gift to you and your baby, and I hope you'll accept them with my compliments.

P.P. S. If you simply can't find time to come in this month, call my office and let me send you the report by mail. It could be very important to your child's health.

As you can imagine, that letter brought a flood of new patients into Dr. Smith's office. The simple act of educating all of those new parents to the fact that they should get their baby's teeth checked turned hundreds of "*suspects*" into prospects.

Of course, lots of times you don't have access to your "*suspects*" names and addresses. But even in those cases, you can use the same basic technique very successfully.

For example:

Suppose you were a doctor, lawyer, accountant, stockbroker, insurance agent, real estate agent, or any other service provider, you still need to educate your "*suspects*" into becoming prospects.

Write a special report
about your services.

Use this report to teach people how to use your services in ways that they would not otherwise think of.

Give the report away free to anyone who might be a "*suspect*" for your services.

Write it in a non threatening, informative style. Teach the reader everything that he or she would want to know in order to make a buying decision, but don't make the report a "*hard sell.*"

Teach them about all of the options, even those that you may not offer. Explain the pros and cons of each. Don't use technical jargon, but don't talk down to them either.

If you're in a retail business, you can still use the same technique.

Freddy uses a "Special Report" to convince
wary public to try hot new high-tech discovery.

Suppose you sell video equipment. You might write a report called *"The Home Video Guide To Better Home Movies."*

A Jeep dealer might do a report called *"37 Great Places To Go Four Wheeling Within 30 Miles Of (insert your home town)"*

Let's look at one more related technique to use education to convert *"suspects"* into prospects.

Put on a series of FREE Seminars.

Place a small ad in your local paper announcing an important seminar on a subject relating to your business.

It could be about specific investments, how to buy local real estate for less, how to live a longer, healthier life, how to make yourself lawsuit proof, how to shoot home video, how to decorate your home for peanuts, gourmet microwave cooking, or anything else. Use your imagination.

Anyway, the ad should explain some of the benefits that the seminar attendees will gain by attending.

It should build your credibility as an expert in the field. Mention your years of experience, or areas of special study, or industry awards, or that you've published articles in various trade journals, or anything else that helps establish you as the expert.

You might even bring in some other, non-competing industry experts to help.

When you present the seminar, have plenty of handouts, or reports, or home study guides to give the attendees.

Most importantly, keep it educational, don't turn it into a two hour sales pitch, or you'll simply irritate the attendees.

At the end of the seminar, thank them for coming, and offer to stay for a while and personally answer any additional questions.

Make certain to collect and maintain the names and addresses of all attendees. That's where the money will come in down the road.

Educating 303

Here's where it really counts. Now that your educating 101 and 202 have brought you tons of new customers, you must continue to maintain an open line of communication with them.

You should call or write them often. You should continue to show them that you are working hard for their business.

When a new product comes out, send them advance notice and offer them a special introductory offer.

Whenever you hear of a new use for your product or service, send them a letter explaining how they can take advantage of it to further increase the value of doing business with you.

If you sell consumables, offer to set them up on an automatic monthly reorder system so they don't have to worry about running out.

If you are in an industry like a lawn care service, or a pool service, or rug cleaning, or pest control, offer to put them on an automatic service call basis and give them a discount for subscribing.

When you have an overstock situation, do a "*private*" sale for past customers only and give them incredible discounts to help you move your excess inventory.

Set up a "*Call The President*" hot line where customers who need special attention can call you quickly and easily. Of course, when you do this, write to them and tell them all about this great new service.

In short, use every opportunity you can find to keep communicating with your customers and continually teach them about all of the things you do to take better care of them than anyone else.

Another great way to communicate with your customers is through a newsletter.

This works particularly well if you are in a fast-paced industry which constantly has new developments.

If you publish a newsletter, write it much the same way as you would a special report, except break it down to smaller bites.

A side benefit of a newsletter is that if you do a really good job in writing it, you may find that people will be willing to actually pay to subscribe to it. If this happens, you'll be able to develop it into another profit center.

By the way, you could also use a newsletter to develop leads, but you should still put a reasonable cover price on it. This way it will carry a higher level of perceived value when you give complimentary subscriptions to your *"suspects."*

**Remember, the only way to keep your
customers is to keep communicating with them.**

And if you mess up, own up to it immediately. Tell the customer what went wrong, what steps you are taking to correct the situation, and how you'll see to it that it doesn't happen again.

Perhaps a shipment arrived too late for you to process the order, or maybe you ran out of whatever the customer ordered. But, always tell the customer the truth.

Most people are quite understanding, and will always give you another chance. If you can, give this customer some compensation for any inconvenience you've caused.

Maybe you could add a special discount, or offer a special deal on another product. Whatever you can do, do it. It will come back to you in spades.

This brings us to the next *"secret."* This important concept is called *"Tell Them Why, And Then They'll Buy."* It's closely related to educating your customer, but it's so important, it deserves it's own section.

The Sixth Secret:

Tell Them WHY, And Then They'll BUY!

People can come up with dozens of different excuses not to buy from you, but most of them are really just smoke screens.

The fact is, there are only three reasons that prospects don't buy from you...

First, they may not want
or need what you're selling.

If this is the case, you shouldn't be *"talking"* to them anyway. Remember the third *secret,* *"Why Talk To Just Anybody When You Could Be Selling Somebody."*

Always target your marketing to reach only your legitimate prospects.

The second reason why they might not buy is...

They truly can't afford what you're selling.

This one only counts if it's true, and they're not just using it as a convenient excuse. If it really is true, you shouldn't be wasting your time or resources on them either. To do so would be like trying to squeeze blood from a rock.

There's only one other reason why people don't buy, and it's the subject of this *"secret."*

They simply don't believe you.

You haven't established enough credibility with your prospects. And one of the best, most effective ways to establish this credibility is to let them in on your inside secrets.

Let them in on your thinking; your rationale. Let them in on the *"reason why"* you're doing what you're doing.

Most businesses try to keep everything about their business a big secret. They don't want anyone to know the inside workings of their operation.

Often, they're more concerned about their competitors finding out something (which the competitors probably already know), than they are about using it to their advantage to get more customers.

In reality, it's these very "secrets" that would entice a customer to want to do business with them in the first place.

If you are offering a product at a
particularly low price, tell your prospects why.

And tell them the truth.

Don't try to make it sound like you're slashing your prices just because you're *"a nice guy,"* or that you're doing it simply because *"you like them."* They won't believe you. You run a business... not *"The Mickey Mouse Club."*

Maybe you are severely overstocked on this item and you need to get rid of some to make room for something else. If that's the case, tell them.

Maybe you have a thousand summer widgets and the summer is over so you need move them or store them for a year. If that's the case, tell the customers.

Tell them that the cost to store these widgets would add another 20% to what you've already invested in them, therefore, you'd rather sell them all right now at a deep discount. In fact, you'll sell them for 10% *below* your cost. By doing so, your customers will get an extraordinary value, and you'll come out better too.

Perhaps you have to make a major bank payment and business has been off so you're having an emergency sale. Don't be embarrassed, tell them.

Maybe your product is less expensive because of a slight manufacturing flaw. Tell your prospects all about it.

Tell them how the flaw is barely noticeable, and that without it, this product would sell for twice the price. Tell them how fortunate they are to get such a great bargain on an otherwise perfect product. Tell them the reason why.

If your price is lower because you have lower overhead, don't just say: *"Our low overhead means lower prices."* Tell them why.

Maybe your building has been in the family for forty years so you have no lease payment to make every month, or perhaps you're located on an out of the way side street instead of the mall, and pay a much lower rent.

If your low overhead is because you are located in the rural area out of town, tell them that. You might point out in your ads that the average rent is X dollars per square foot in the city, but that you only pay Y dollars. Therefore each item you sell reflects that savings.

If you are making a special introductory offer to get people to try you for the first time, say so.

Tell them that once they try your product or service they'll fall in love with it and keep using it. Therefore, you're willing to sell it at your cost the first time, or even provide a free sample, just to get them to try you once. Whatever the reason, tell them.

If you are offering a special deal because you just bought a large shipment of factory closeouts, tell them how the price for these goods is usually X dollars, but that you just bought the entire final production run from the factory, so you got them for much less.

Tell your prospects that instead of pricing these closeouts at your normal price and making twice your normal profit, you'd rather use them to help move some other item in which you are currently overstocked. Explain that for every one of the slower moving items they buy, you'll let them have one of the closeouts at half price.

How about this one? We once saw a small company that ran a quarter page ad once a week, and their larger competitor, that sold the same goods, ran *three* full page ads every week. Guess what the smaller company said in their ads?

We sell the exact same goods as XYZ Company, but we sell them for less.

How can we sell the same products for less than our much larger competitor?

Simple. They run a full page ad three times a week in our local paper. That ad costs X dollars.

Multiply that times three, and it comes up to a tidy sum.

But we, on the other hand, only spend Y dollars on this small ad, once a week. And that means that our average price can be 11% lower than theirs.

The best part about it was that they actually put the exact numbers and percentages in the ad. It was so detailed and specific, that you couldn't help but believe it.

If your prices are *higher*, tell them the reason why.

Maybe it's because your widget lasts 10 times longer than the average widget so you back it with a lifetime guarantee; or that your widget requires less maintenance, or has lower operating costs which saves X dollars over its life so that it actually ends up costing its owner less to use.

If your prices are a little higher because you have three times the service or support staff, and provide a higher level of service, tell them that.

Explain that your prices are 5% higher than your competitors, but explain the superior level of service that you provide. Maybe you make house calls, or include regular maintenance at no additional cost, or provide on site training. Show them how, for a few cents more, they can save time, effort, and frustration by shopping with you.

Sure, it costs a little bit more, but look at all this power!

If your prices are higher because you can respond to a service call in two hours instead of the six hours that your competitors take, tell them.

Remind them of the cost of *"down time,"* and all of the other things they could be doing during that four hour difference.

Always tell them the reason why you are doing something and your prospects will probably believe you. But as always, tell the truth.

Here's a perfect example of a case where the true reason why (although slightly embarrassing), allowed us to turn a potentially devastating situation into an incredibly profitable one.

Back when we were in the electronics business, each of our five video stores had a huge movie rental club. And part of the movie club was a section of adult movies.

At the beginning of the video age, a large segment of the market wanted the ability to rent these tapes and watch them in the privacy of their own homes.

We carefully and discreetly met this *"want"* without offending those who did not wish to see these tapes.

Anyway, this part of our business started to decline as more and more family fare became available on video tape. Also, at about the same time, quite a stir was building about pornography, and a *"grass roots"* movement against adult video rentals was gaining momentum.

A few Congressmen had even introduced some quite restrictive legislation to help curtail it.

We felt that the *"handwriting was on the wall,"* and decided that we should get out of that part of the business.

The problem was that we had about 8,000 adult tapes in our inventory. This represented a significant investment (each tape cost us between $30-$70 and retailed for $60-$120).

We decided to run a full page ad explaining our situation and offering the tapes at a deep discount.

Take a look at the headline and some excerpts from that ad...

Why Would Antin's Sell
$100 Movies For Only $14.99?

I'm writing to alert you to an embarrassing situation, but first you must agree not to laugh or be offended by the subject matter because frankly, it's a little bit unusual and a little bit of a "Hot Potato."

IT'S ADULT MOVIES... now don't laugh; you promised!

My brother, Alan, and I have an embarrassing and frustrating problem that we would like to share with you both in confidence and in the form of an opportunity.

First, the problem: There are a bunch of people in Congress who are hell bent on doing away with your rights as they affect

things like Adult Movies and magazines.

I'm not saying that adult movies are good or bad, only that people should have the right to make their own choices.

That notwithstanding, the truth of the matter is that some heavyweights in Congress have introduced legislation that's going to make it illegal to rent adult movies.

That really ticks me off, not so much about not being able to rent adult tapes, because frankly, that's a matter of personal preference, but with all of the scandals in Washington, they should get their own house in order before they mess with yours!

Nevertheless, we have a real problem. Besides taking away some of everybody's rights, they're going to take away about 8,000 of our movies! We've got to decide what to do before that occurs...

We could sell our entire adult library to the greedy, unscrupulous exporters who, like vultures flying over an opportunity, are trying to get tapes that sell for $60-$120 for only $15 or $20.

This is horrifying to us because these tapes are in great condition and are worth a lot more than that. Besides, they include some of the best adult tapes ever made.

Before I go any further, I'd like to say that over the last couple of months, Alan and I have talked a lot about a way to better acknowledge you, our valued customers, and convey to you how much we truly appreciate all of the business you've done with us... and the purchases you've made... and all of the friends you've referred to us.

We thought about a charming little card, and almost had one written, or giving you a discount coupon, but maybe a better way to do it is to pass on a savings to you of a very unusual sort where you could save up to seventy dollars on a hundred dollar value; and even find a way to give you a FREE adult movie because...

If we must suffer the indignation of losing $70 per tape on our entire adult inventory, it's far better to lose it in the form of a special consideration to you, our valued customer than to some vulturous exporter whom we'll probably never deal with again.

We feel that the "good will" we'll accrue if we sell a million dollars worth of tapes to you for 15 or 20 cents on the dollar will help lessen the loss.

So for the next three days, the people who we really cherish; who have contributed the most to our success; and to whom we owe a great debt of gratitude will be afforded the opportunity to buy any of the adult tapes in our library for...

Not the seventy dollars we paid for many of them...

Not for half... or even half again...

But for only $14.99 each!

And as a special bonus inducement to help us take the pain as quickly as possible so we can move on with our lives, we'll even give you one tape of your choice absolutely free for every five adult tapes you buy.

The ad went on about the incredible selection, mentioned some of the titles, reemphasized that we hoped that the nature of the ad didn't offend them, and apologized if it did, and included a coupon that the customer could redeem to get the special offer of buy five, get one FREE.

Did you notice how we truthfully explained our problem in such a way as to tell the reader exactly why we were making such an incredible offer?

By the way, at the very same time that we ran that ad, another dealer was trying to sell his adult tapes. He ran an ad too. But his ad simply listed a bunch of the titles of his tapes with their prices.

Here's the amazing part... His prices were even lower than ours!

Why is that amazing?

Well, merely by explaining our problem and the reason for the sale in that one ad, we sold all of our adult tapes in just a few days. That one ad generated over a hundred thousand dollars practically overnight.

But the real kicker was that the other dealer (in spite of his lower prices), was having trouble moving his tapes. In fact, he asked us if we would sell *his tapes* to our customers on consignment. He said he would bring them over to our stores, and that we could keep half of everything we got for them.

That ad turned out to be one of the single most responsive promotions in the history of our electronics stores. And since all of our adult tapes had been in the rental library, they had already been written off on our taxes. This meant that we had no current cost of goods in the promotion. The revenue it generated was pure profit. So, not only was the promotion responsive, it was also quite profitable.

All because we told the reason why!

When you don't tell the reason why, your prospects will be more concerned with trying to figure out your ulterior motive than with honestly considering the purchase.

And that can rob you of thousands of dollars of sales.

Of course, even when you do tell the reason why, customers and prospects still feel a certain amount of risk when they do business with you; especially for the first time.

But as you might have guessed, we're about to show you how to handle that with ease. Let's look at the next "*secret*"...

The Seventh Secret:

Put Your Money Where Your Mouth Is!

How often have you heard (or even said) *"Put your money where your mouth is,"* or *"Prove it,"* or *"Show me"*?

Well, your prospects are saying it too.

In droves.

It's simply human nature to be a little bit skeptical. And these days, it's even more common than ever.

American consumers are sick of false claims, bogus offers, and hyped-up products that sound great in advertising but fall far short of their promises.

They've grown tired of being taken for suckers, and they've become much more savvy in making their purchases.

Forget about what P.T. Barnum said, *"There's a sucker born every minute."*

The business person who relies on that and tries to flimflam his customers will soon find out that it's really he or she that's been the *"sucker."*

Consumers not only want proof of your claims, they also want to know what happens when your product doesn't live up to them.

They perceive (rightfully) that all of the risk of the business transaction rests solely with them.

They look at it this way.

They're going to trade you their hard earned money (a known certainty), for your products or services (that may or *may not* perform as promised).

They figure that you have no risk once you get the money. After all, money is money. It's nothing more, and nothing less.

But, you're giving them something that is not so cut and dried. You're giving them the promise of some benefit or advantage that if realized, *may* be worth the money they gave you.

And if those particular benefits are not realized... if they don't come true, they've lost their hard earned money.

When you understand this concept of the risk that a prospect feels in doing business with you, and you make an effort to reduce (or even reverse) it, you'll see your sales skyrocket.

This is actually fairly easy to do, but only if you really do provide an honest, valuable product or service that does, in fact, live up to your claims.

If that's the case, this new consumer attitude is actually a tremendous opportunity.

Let's look at some ways to capitalize on it.

First, offer a guarantee.

We're not talking about the manufacturer's warranty that may come with the products that you sell. That typically only promises to repair or replace defective items.

At the point of purchase, the customer is more concerned about *"defective promises,"* than defective items.

Offer a guarantee such that if the product fails to perform as you promised, or that your level of service is not what you promised, the customer can get his or her money back.

This way, you'll show the customer that you have enough faith in your product (or service) that you're willing to shoulder the risk of the transaction.

Your guarantee might say...

"If this product (or service) fails to perform as we've promised, return it for a full refund."

This will go a long way towards knocking down the *"risk barrier"* that might be keeping the prospect from becoming a customer.

But wait a minute...

This kind of guarantee, while better than none, really doesn't have enough teeth for many wary prospects.

A lot of people might still be reluctant to buy, because they wonder if your perception of your performance promises and their level of expected performance are the same.

Who is to be the judge of whether or not the product or service is living up to your promises?

Why not simply put more teeth into your guarantee?

Make it *"Iron-Clad"* from the customer's point of view.

After all, that's the only point of view that matters when it comes to making a sale.

What do I mean by *"Iron-Clad?"* Simple. Forget the fine print!

Make your guarantee plain, simple, and take all of the guess work and speculation out of it. Say something like:

"If, after you purchase this product, you feel, for any reason, that it fails to live up to our promises, simply bring it back to us and we'll immediately and cheerfully give you a 100% refund of the purchase price. No questions asked!"

Do you see how far a guarantee like this goes towards eliminating the prospect's perception of the risk of doing business with you?

Of course, some prospects might not be exactly sure of what they want. Deep down inside, they're worried that even if the product does fully live up to your promises, they may end up unhappy with their own purchase decision.

*Archeologists discover irrefutable evidence proving
the cave was indeed inhabited during the "Iron-Age."*

Maybe you should add something in your guarantee that even protects them from making a poor buying decision.

That would make it stronger yet, wouldn't it?

Suppose you even protected the customer from his *own* mistakes. That would further reduce his perceived risk, wouldn't it?

Why not modify your *"Iron-Clad"* Guarantee to cover his mistakes as well.

"If, after you purchase this product, you feel, for any reason, that it fails to live up to our promises (or even if it does and you just change your mind), simply bring it back to us and we'll immediately and cheerfully give you a 100% refund of the purchase price. No questions asked!"

Remember, the goal is to remove the customer's perceived risk of doing business with you.

Now you might be thinking that if you offer such a comprehensive guarantee, some of the customers will use it to take advantage of you... That some of them will try to "*rip you off.*"

If so, you're absolutely right. A small percentage of them will. A *very small* percentage.

And when it happens, simply chalk it up to a cost of doing business. Just like your rent, electric bill, or any other part of your overhead.

But guess what...

This part of your overhead is actually a brilliant investment.

Chances are, that for every dollar this strategy costs you because of someone taking advantage of you, you'll make ten or twenty dollars in profit from the additional sales it generates.

Whatever you do, don't let your ego get involved. Even when you know that the customer is trying to "*rip you off,*" don't take it personally.

The losses from that small percentage won't even begin to compare with the massive windfall of new-found profits generated by the multitude of additional honest customers that you'll attract.

What else could you do to reduce or eliminate this perceived risk?

Well, regardless of which kind of guarantee you offer, or how strong you feel it is, try lengthening it.

If the industry standard guarantee in your field is 30 days, make yours 60 or 90 days.

If industry standard is 90 days, make yours six months or a year.

Don't worry too much about the added exposure, because if your product or service is really good, it shouldn't give you too many more problems.

But the added sales will add a chunk to your bottom line.

Of course, if you sell a product or service that never breaks down (such as books, tapes, clothes, art, in fact, anything non-mechanical), there's a major side benefit to extending your guarantee.

The longer people have to do something, the greater likelihood that they will forget to do it.

In other words, if you sell something with a short money-back guarantee, the buyer feels a certain amount of pressure to immediately give the product a quick look, and make a snap decision *before* his guarantee expires!

You can forget about them giving you any benefit of the doubt.

In this case... "Maybe" means "NO!"

But if you sell the same item, and give the buyers a long guarantee, they don't feel any pressure to make a snap decision. They will take their time, and frequently give you the benefit of the doubt.

In this case... "Maybe" often ends up being "YES!"

You see, since they now have the luxury of all of that extra time to "*think about it,*" making a decision becomes a relatively low priority.

Frequently (in fact, most of the time) they will forget about the time limit, and won't think of the money back guarantee until it has long expired.

Don't get us wrong here. We do not recommend or condone in any way that you use this technique to trick people into getting stuck with your products or services.

If you do, it will end up costing you far more down the road. You'll understand this more fully when we get to "*secret*" number twelve.

Actually, if a customer decides that they want their money back even *after* the guarantee has expired, you should probably give it to them.

Maybe not always, but you should certainly hear them out, try to make them happy, and, if necessary, honestly consider refunding their purchase price.

It's usually good business to do so.

Now, if you really want to supercharge your profits, take the next step...

Instead of just removing the risk, *reverse* it.

Show the customer that not only are you totally eliminating all of his perceived risk in doing business with you, but you are also taking all of the risk of the transaction yourself.

One way to do this is to offer them credit.

Tell them that they don't have to pay for the product until they've had it for 30 days.

Prove to them that you trust them, and they'll practically be compelled to trust you.

Try the "Puppy Dog" Close, or the "Sale On Approval"

It's actually quite powerful, and is based on the belief that once the customer has your product, or starts enjoying your service, they'll decide that they can't live without it.

Simply let them take the product home and start using it. Tell them to take it for the weekend (without paying for it) and if, on Monday morning, they decide they don't want to keep it, simply bring it back and they'll owe you nothing.

What this basically does is tell the customers that they can try your product or service with absolutely no risk at all.

One of the old advertising masters used to tell a story about buying a horse...

Two men brought horses to show him. Both of the men told him how great their horses were. Both of them bragged about the gentleness of their horses.

Both men pointed out the fine health that their horses were in, and that they had years of productive life ahead of them.

Both men spoke of what a terrific value their horses were.

But here's where they differed.

One of the men said "*Look, why not take the horse for a week. If you don't find it satisfactory, come back, and I'll return your money.***"**

The second man said, "*Look, I know what a fine horse this is and I'd like to prove it to you. Don't give me any money now, but take the horse and try it for a week. In that time, you'll see for yourself that what I say is true. Then come back and pay me for the horse.***"**

Needless to say, he bought the second man's horse.

The concept of risk reversal
is quite powerful, indeed.

Just like the man with the second horse, you know that *your* product more than lives up to its promises, therefore, most of these new-found sales (that you probably would have otherwise not made in the first place) will stick.

Remember, the farther you go towards making the prospect feel that he's not risking anything by doing business with you, the better off you'll be.

We already saw how to reduce the risk with a basic guarantee.

We saw how to practically eliminate the risk with an "*Iron-Clad Guarantee.*"

And then we saw how to actually *reverse* the risk with the sale on approval technique.

But what else can you do to make the customer even more comfortable and more eager to say yes?

Try Bonusing!

Adding a bonus serves two important functions. The first, and more obvious of the two, is that it increases the prospect's perceived value of the entire deal.

After all, who doesn't want to get more for their money?

A bonus is anything that you can add in to *"sweeten the deal."* It could be additional products or services, or any other consideration.

Here's where you need to be creative. You need to find several low cost, but high perceived value things, that you can use to give the customer that something extra.

Our favorite bonus product is information. You can add tremendous value with information, and the cost is next to nothing.

For example, write a Special Report, or produce a video.

Make it meaty. Make it a *"tell all."* Make it a true value.

Suppose you sell camcorders. Produce a video that teaches customers how to shoot better home video. Or 101 new ways to use a camcorder.

If you sell microwave ovens, publish a special recipe book.

If you're an accountant, write a report that teaches year 'round tax savings. Point out that the secrets contained in your report will allow the client to save far more than what your total bill for the year will be.

If you sell suits and jackets, give them a free garment bag or a $10 dollar discount for dry cleaning.

Remember, what is natural to you... the things about your business or industry that you take for granted... the tricks of the trade, if you will... can be quite valuable to your customers.

Don't worry about giving your secrets away, if your product or service has value, it can only increase sales. This ties in with *"secret"* number five, *"The Value Of A Good Education."*

If you do write a special report, make sure to put a cover price on it. Price it at $19.95, $39.95, or even $99; whatever is consistent with the subject matter.

Of course, you could use just about anything for a bonus, but no matter what you use, make sure to establish a definite value for the bonus.

If you don't educate the customer about the tremendous value that you are giving them FREE, it won't carry any weight. And any advantage that could have been gained will be lost.

If you sell consumables, give them a little bit more for the same price.

You've heard the term
"A Bakers Dozen," haven't you?

Well, that's a perfect example of bonusing.

Suppose you were going to buy a dozen doughnuts, and you could buy them from either of two local bakeries.

Both of these bakeries make fine doughnuts.

But at one of them you pay for 12 doughnuts and you get 12doughnuts, and at the other bakery, you pay for 12 doughnuts and get 13 *(a bakers dozen)*.

Which bakery would you be inclined to patronize?

Here's another example.

One of the authors, Brad Antin, lives in a beach community, and one of his favorite foods is blackened shrimp.

All along the beach there are several small seafood restaurants, and of course, they all have blackened shrimp on their menus.

Brad's community, like most beach communities, relies on tourism for its economy, so the restaurants are quite competitive.

Most of them offer a blackened shrimp dinner that comes with six large shrimp, however, one of these restaurants serves eight shrimp on their dinner plate.

Which of these restaurants do you think Brad patronizes most often?

Why not use that same
concept in *your* business?

If you own a grocery store, or a market, use this concept when selling produce or baked goods.

If you sell a product that uses consumables, use the bonusing concept to generate future sales.

For example, if you sell a low priced item that uses consumables, you might give it away in order to generate all of the future sales of the consumable.

You know, *"Give them the razor, to sell the razor blades."*

If you sell a high priced item, do the opposite. Give them an introductory supply of all of the consumables when they first buy the main item.

Now, for the *ultimate* in risk reversal!

Use the *"Better Than Risk Free Guarantee."*

It's really quite simple. Here's how it works...

Combine a no risk, *"Iron-Clad"* guarantee that allows the prospect to return the purchase for any or no reason, with a valuable bonus, but with one delightful twist.

They get to keep the bonus even if
they return the product for a full refund!

Talk about powerful!

Imagine the impact your ads will have on your prospects when you teach them all about your product or service, and you show them all of the benefits and advantages that they'll realize with your product (using the techniques you've already learned here).

By now, they're just about ready to say YES.

Then they get to the part about the valuable bonus. They look at it and start to realize what a great value your offer really is. Far better than any other they've seen.

Now, you've got them seriously thinking about whipping out the check book...

Then they get to the guarantee which says...

"Better Than Risk-Free Guarantee!"

"If, after you purchase this product, you feel, for any reason, that it fails to live up to our promises (or even if it does and you just change your mind), simply bring it back to us and we'll immediately and cheerfully give you a 100% refund of the purchase price. No questions asked!"

But even if you do decide to return this product for a full refund, please keep the FREE bonus as our special gift to you. It's our way of simply thanking you for at least giving us a try!

This way, even if you decide that it's not right for you, the worst that can happen is you'll get a $50 value absolutely FREE. That's BETTER THAN RISK FREE!

An offer like this is almost impossible for a qualified prospect to ignore.

When you understand and use the concept of risk reversal to your advantage, you'll become virtually unstoppable in your market area.

And as long as your product or service is an honest value, the only outcome will be profits almost beyond belief.

The Only Votes That Count Are The Ones That Are Bought And Paid For!

No, we are not about to suggest that you engage in graft or corruption.

We're not talking about stuffing a ballot box.

We're talking about something far more profitable than that...

Once you start applying the elements of good marketing to all of your advertising efforts, you'll see an immediate increase in sales.

And of course, this means that your customer acquisition cost will drop like a rock.

So instead of spending $50 or $100 for each new customer you generate from your ads, you may find that by using these techniques you get it down to half, a third, or even a tenth of that.

And, that's the ultimate form of leverage.

In other words, let's say you now spend $1,000 on an ad that brings in 10 customers. The cost of attracting each of these customers is $100 ($1,000 divided by 10). But what if you start using what you've learned here, and run an ad that cost the same $1,000, but generates 100 customers. These customers now only cost you $10 each ($1,000 divided by 100). That's a thousand percent increase.

Most people, when they produce an ad that generates far more business than what they're used to, tend to get quite excited. Can you blame them?

Many of them immediately raise their ad budget so they can pull in more and more customers.

They usually start to run bigger ads, and run them more often.

That's OK, but before you go hog wild, answer this one question...

How high is up?

In other words, let's say you use these techniques to develop your next ad.

Suppose this new ad brings in ten times the customers of any other ad you've ever run.

That's great, isn't it?

Maybe, and maybe not. In this "*secret*," we're going to look at a way to reduce your customer acquisition cost even further... so you can make even more money.

What if a different headline, or different offer, or different price point would have generated 20, 50, or 100 times the response of that one.

You never know what will pull the best, until you test it.

Sure, you can follow our basic guidelines. That will get you started down the right road. That will keep you going in the right direction.

But you should always look at every ad, every sales letter, every headline, every offer, and even every sales pitch as nothing more than one step in an ongoing process.

Remember the fourth *secret, "Don't Let Your Advertising Be All Show And No Go!"*

That's where you learned that direct response advertising was much more effective than image advertising.

Well, you should also remember that direct response marketing (by it's very nature), provides you with a way to *track the effectiveness* of every ad you run.

And while we're on the subject of tracking your ads, make sure you set up a log book to keep track of the specifics of each ad.

Every ad, every sales letter, every promotional piece you run should be coded with an extension number, department number, operator number, or some other code number so you can identify which ad generated which sales.

The log should include any information that might be important later. It should at least have a copy of the ad, the code number, the date it ran, the results it generated, the placement in the paper or magazine or the TV station, time, and show that it aired on.

This is very important, because once you run a successful ad, you'll know in dollars and cents just how successful it was.

Now, your goal is to come up with an even better ad.

So you sit down and write a new ad and show it to your employees and associates.

When they tell you how wonderful it is, you commit a fortune to build an entire campaign around this new masterpiece, right?

Wrong... Wrong... Wrong!

The people who tell you how great your ad is, are usually just telling you what they think you want to hear.

And get this...

They are not the ones who you want to respond to the ad.

No, the only way to determine the effectiveness of an ad is to put it to a vote by the only people whose opinions matter...

Your customers!

And the way they vote is with their pocketbooks!

They may call and tell you how wonderful an ad was, but if they don't buy, it doesn't count.

Your trade organization may give you an award for a great ad, but that, too, doesn't count.

You may get thousands of people to call and request more

information, but if they don't actually *buy something*, it doesn't count.

The only votes that count are when somebody buys something. That's it. Nothing else matters.

Brilliant marketing wizard invents the "Market-Test"
to select a name for the newest sandwich sensation.

So how do you come up with the best possible ads? By testing.

What do you test?

Everything.

Test your headlines...

Test your offers...

Test your guarantees...

Test your price points...

Test your sales letters...

Test your in-person sales pitches...

Test your back-end offers...

Test different media (newspapers, magazines, card decks, mailing lists, radio stations, or TV stations)...

Test... Test... Test!

Here's how it works.

First, you run an ad that you believe should pull well. This becomes your starting point.

Let's call it your *"control"* ad.

Track the results of this ad and figure out what your customer acquisition cost is, or your cost per dollar sales.

Let's say you normally run the ad three, four, or five times.

Why not try a different headline on the ad for one or two of those times, and see if the results change.

But only do this if the two ads that you're comparing are otherwise identical, and they run on the same day of the week.

If you test one ad against another, and you change more than one factor (such as headline, copy, offer, price, etc.), the results become almost meaningless.

If you test more than one factor at a time, you'll never really know which of the items made the difference in the results.

Another great way to test two different headlines (or any other single factor in an ad) is to do a *"split-run."* Many newspapers and magazines will allow you to run two versions of your ad in the same issue.

They'll print half (or some other fraction) of their circulation with one version and the other half with the other version.

This is a great way to determine if a test ad will beat your control ad. Simply track the results from each ad.

They could go up, or they could go down.

If they go down on the test ad, it means that your control (the ad with the first headline) is stronger than the test.

If they go up, that means the test headline is stronger than the control.

Repeat the test.

If the test ad beats the control again, then the test ad should become your new control, and develop another test to compare it to.

That's a simple look at testing.

Even if you don't have a very big ad budget, you should still test for a better headline.

Here's another technique. Look at the classified ad section of the paper or of one of your favorite magazines. Notice how most classified ads read like headlines.

That's because they both have to perform the same function.

A classified ad has only a few words to get the reader to take some form of action (usually call or write for more information).

Well, the same is true for the headline of a space ad (that's an ad where you purchase a certain amount of space in a newspaper or magazine). In a space ad, the headline has only a few words to convince the reader to read the rest of the ad.

This similarity allows you to use cheap little classified ads to test several headlines.

Write four or five headlines that you want to test. Next, place them in the form of classified ads.

For example, if you were selling a diet or exercise plan, you might try something like...

How to lose 20 pounds of fat in 30 days without dieting. For information, call 555-1234. Ask for ext. 101.

**Amazing new non-diet melts 20 pounds off the average adult
in only 30 days. For information, call 555-1234. Ask for ext.
202.**

**Doctor discovers way to eat all you want and still lose weight
For information, call 555-1234. Ask for ext. 303.**

**Make your friends jealous with your new slim, trim figure.
For information, call 555-1234. Ask for ext. 404.**

Run these classified ads in your local paper, and carefully track
the number of calls that each one gets.

If one of them generates significantly more responses than the
others, you can almost bet that it will work better as a headline for a
space ad, too.

How's that for a down and dirty, cheap way to test your
headlines?

Suppose you run classified ads that cost you $200, and you find
out that one of the headlines increases response to your main ad by
10%.

Say your control ad brought in 50 customers who, over the years,
will each do about $3,000 of business with you.

If this little $200 test points you to a new headline that increases
response by only 10%, that means that you got five more customers
for the same marketing cost. That works out to an additional $15,000
in sales for a $200 investment.

That's what we call leverage.

Of course, you won't always get a 10% increase in response.
Sometimes the test won't beat the control at all. But then again, it's
not unusual for one headline to out pull another by as much as 10, 15,
or even 20 times!

Remember, you never know how high is up unless you test.

Again, you should test everything. We've seen a simple little change of price make a huge difference in response.

Sometimes, on the same product, $19.95 might out-pull $21.95 by many times. Or $29.95 might out-pull $19.95. That's right; the lowest price doesn't necessarily pull the best response.

Wouldn't it be great if testing showed that you could increase your price (which increases your profit per sale), *and* increase your number of sales all at the same time?

Well, that just might be the case, so...

Test... Test... Test!

If you have a retail store, or have salespeople who go out to see clients, or a telemarketing staff, you should have frequent sales meetings to keep track of what elements of the pitch seem to be working, and which don't. Trade this information among the sales force.

Have different sales people test different sales pitches. Chances are good that you'll be able to use testing to fine tune your basic sales presentations and see an immediate increase in your closing rate.

Test everything. We can not overemphasize this.

Test ad placement. Does your ad pull better in the general news section of the paper, or the business section, or the sports section? Find out.

Which *"hot-button,"* or benefit about your product, when explained in your ads, creates the most sales? Test it.

We usually like to spend about 85% of our marketing budget on our control ads, and save 15% of the budget for testing.

Often, that 15% doesn't generate enough sales to even break even, but it's a fairly cheap way to get some very important information.

But the real pay-off is when a new test ad *does* out-pull the control.

Even if it's only by a small margin, when it becomes the new control, the increase in sales more than makes up for the few losers in the testing process.

If you use direct mail to sell your goods and services, test different mailing lists.

Rent the minimum number of names that the list manager will allow, and mail only a couple of thousand letters.

Some lists will generate 10 or 20 times the number of sales per thousand letters mailed as other lists.

Once you find a truly hot list, then, and only then, should you mail to the whole list; not all at once, though. You should actually test a bigger sample, then a bigger one yet, and so on and so forth.

But don't stop there. Test another list, and another, and another.

But what about the letter itself? Test different colors of paper, ink, and different type styles.

Test different sizes and types of paper and envelopes. Test different order forms, guarantees, and response methods.

Do your customers prefer to call an (800) number to order, or would they rather write? Do they prefer to pay by check or credit card? Can you increase orders by allowing C.O.D., or even spread the payments out over a few months?

You can even do a version of a split-run test with a mailing list.

Say you rent 5,000 names. Mail one version of the letter to the first, third, fifth, seventh, etc. name and the other version to the second, fourth, sixth, eighth, etc. name. This means that half of the list (at random) will get one version of the letter, and the others will get another version.

There's only one way to find out what works best...

Test... Test... Test.

But remember: Change only one factor at a time. This is critical to the success of your test.

We've pointed out some of the obvious things you should test, but don't limit your testing to just these.

You should test everything.

Every facet of your marketing, sales, and customer service that you could do more than one way should be tested.

Let the marketplace tell you with their dollars which is the best way to go.

Let them vote with their dollars which offer is best, or which headline is best, or which sales pitch is best.

Now let's look at the next *"secret."* This concept deals with who actually *"sees"* your advertising.

The Ninth Secret:

Life (and business) Is A Big Parade!

This is an extremely easy "*secret*" to understand, but for some reason, it's one of the most often ignored "*secrets*" of all.

The basic concept is this.

Most business people promiscuously change their advertising just because they themselves get sick of seeing it.

And, what's even worse, they do this even when the ad that they are dropping is still pulling better than any other ad they've tested.

That's silly, isn't it?

After all, you already know that the only factor that matters in your advertising (aside from being honest and ethical) is whether or not it is generating more sales than any other ad.

Well, if it is...

Don't change it!

Hold on, now. We're not contradicting what we just taught you about testing.

We're not saying that you should only run one ad until the results totally die off.

What we're saying is, that unless one of your test ads beats your control, that control should remain your main focus.

That control should get the lion's share of your ad budget. And it should continue to get the lion's share of the budget until a test ad beats it.

Then, and only then, should you change your control.

Sure, you'll get sick of seeing the same ad time after time.

Sure, your employees will get sick of that same old tired ad.

And yes, even some of your customers will tell you that they're sick of that same old ad.

But don't change it until you've got something better.

Upon buying the circus, the ill-fated
brothers try a "different" marketing angle.

Picture a moving parade...

Let's look at this parade from two different vantage points.

First, imagine that you are in the crowd on the street watching the parade go by.

You see a beautiful float sponsored by one company or group, then you see another, then you see a marching band.

Maybe the next thing is a group of horsemen on beautiful white horses followed by a bunch of clowns.

Maybe the clowns are followed by the Shriners in their funny little cars.

All of the paraders are doing a great job of entertaining you, and you can't wait to see what's coming next.

Every new float, marching band, or group is different, exciting, interesting, and fun to watch.

You enjoy the parade from start to finish.

Now, let's change our vantage point. Instead of watching the parade, you're in it. You are riding on a float in the middle of the parade.

You don't see all of the floats in front of and behind you...

You don't see the clowns, or the horsemen, or motorcycles...

You don't see all of the marching bands...

You don't even get to see the Shriners.

You look out into the crowd and see a mass of humanity stretching out for block after block after block.

And, of course, you see your own float.

Pretty soon, it all gets quite boring.

Since you see the crowd as a mass rather than as a group of individuals, you don't even notice how they all smile, and clap when your float goes by.

You start to *notice* little flaws in your float. Maybe a few flowers are missing or the paint is starting to chip.

Then you start to wish you were on a different, more exciting float.

So you wait until you think nobody will notice, and jump off and join the people on the next float.

At the end of the parade, your old float, the one with the missing flowers and the chipped paint is judged to be the best float in the parade, and the people riding that float are awarded the grand prize.

But not you...You jumped ship.

What you failed to realize is that everyone in the crowd only saw your float for a brief moment, and they loved it.

And each block that you drove down brought more and more new (and interested) people to see your float.

The people who saw it only paid attention to it when it was holding their interest.

But you were on the same float for block after block, so you quickly got tired of it.

It's the same thing with your advertising.

Henry Ford once cancelled an ad that he thought the public was sick of... at least *he* was certainly sick of it.

And get this... the ad had *never* run. He had seen it in the planning stages, and had grown tired of it before it ever ran in a single publication.

You (and your staff) will always tire of an ad before your prospects do because you see it every time it runs.

But your prospects only see your ads when they are in the market for what you are selling.

When they're not thinking about your products or services, they don't even notice your ad.

And that's OK, because someone else is coming into the market everyday.

Doesn't it make sense to try and sell them with the most effective ad possible?

Doesn't it make sense that the most effective ad possible (at any given moment) is the one that is your current control?

Look at it this way. No matter what stage of life you are currently going through, you usually notice advertising that is directed at you, and seldom notice the advertising that isn't.

For example, a teenager will usually notice ads for soft drinks, blue jeans, music, tennis shoes, etc.

But how many teenagers notice ads for retirement plans, or disposable diapers, or dentures?

A single adult will usually notice ads for clubs, fashions, cologne or perfume, sports cars, etc.

But single adults are generally blind to ads for toys, children's games, and again, diapers.

A young married couple with toddlers will surely notice ads for diapers, housewares, etc.

But they typically won't pay any attention to ads for retirement homes, supplemental medicare insurance, or investment properties.

Let's say that you own a diaper service. And let's further assume that you develop a terrific control ad that attracts young parents to your service like metal filings are attracted to a magnet.

This ad has all of the elements of a great sales piece. You hit all of the hot buttons, and every young parent reads the ad with the feeling that it was written just for him or her.

So you run this ad again and again.

And you make tons and tons of money.

After a while, you may start to get sick of the ad, and you might be tempted to change it.

But before you do, take a look at the birth announcements of your local paper.

What do you see? That's right, every day, new babies are being born. And that means two things...

First, these new babies are going to need diapers. And secondly, these new babies are making new parents. And these new parents share the same concerns, hopes, and dreams as the new parents of last week, and the week before, and even for many weeks before that.

Of course, as we said in the preface, things have changed over the last several years. And they'll continue to change.

Your control ad may not remain strong and profitable for years and years, but you'll be surprised at just how long it will.

So don't change it unless you already have something that has proven (with actual sales) to beat it.

Otherwise, you'll just be costing yourself a fortune in lost sales.

Just in case you doubt how long some ads can keep pulling, try this little test. Go to your local library and look at some back issues of "Popular Science" or "Popular Mechanics."

Check several issues from each of the last 2, 3, or even 5 years.

Flip through these magazines and notice how many of the ads that you see in issues from several years ago, also appear in some of the current issues.

That should tell you something.

The companies that spend a fortune to run those ads wouldn't keep running them if they were not producing.

Sure, many companies will give an ad more than one chance to prove itself, but nobody is going to run a losing ad for five years.

They wouldn't be able to stay in business that long without sales.

As a final point, when it comes to your advertising, you must be brutally analytical.

Forget the ego.

Forget the image.

Forget everything other than honesty, ethics, and dollars and sense, and your advertising will make money year after year after year.

The Tenth Secret:

Everyone Loves The Circus, But No One Likes To Jump Through Hoops!

Each of the *"secrets"* revealed in this book is quite potent on it's own, but the important thing here is not the individual *"secrets."* It's the way they come together to give you a complete foundation for your marketing strategy.

Up until now, we've uncovered some common sense techniques *(that aren't common knowledge)* which will identify and attract new customers, but that's not the whole picture.

Believe it or not (and we hope you do), convincing hundreds or even thousands of new customers to patronize you for the first time *will not* make you wealthy.

It *might not* even make you successful.

And sometimes, it's *not even enough* to survive on, for the long term.

But take heart, because the *"secrets"* that we'll uncover for you now, and in the next two sections, will give you exactly what you need to really strike it rich.

In fact, let's call these the *"Gold-Mine Secrets!"*

Why the *"Gold-Mine Secrets?"*

You see, the first nine *"secrets"* that we talked about dealt primarily with getting tons of customers to do business with you for the first time.

Look at them as the secrets that help you *"locate the mother lode."*

Discovering gold is one thing and, of course, it's important, but it's only the first step towards success. Next you need to methodically and diligently "*mine the gold.*"

Otherwise, you'll get just a glimpse of success.

It will *seem* to be within reach, but you won't quite be able to grasp it.

So let's go after the "*big nuggets*" in the "*mine,*" and make some real money, OK?

The first of these "*Gold-Mine Secrets,*" deals with customer service.

Stop!

Don't tell us that you've heard it before, so you don't need to study this section.

Don't think that since you don't get a lot of complaints or have to give a lot of refunds that you're doing the right things (or not doing the wrong things).

Don't think that giving good customer service is so obvious and such common sense that we don't need to discuss it.

If you are thinking any of these things, forget it!

Otherwise, you'll be throwing away some extremely valuable, profit-producing concepts and techniques.

This is important, so pay attention.

We're not talking about the typical stuff you've, no doubt, already heard about

"*The customer is always right.*"

Or, "*You should render service with a smile.*"

Or, "*You should follow up and follow through on your claims and promises.*"

These things are all important, but we want you to look for more than just the obvious ways to better serve your customers.

Just in case you do doubt the importance of customer service, let's look at some of the reasons that customers stop doing business with you.

Most companies accept customer attrition as a fact of life. It's just a cost of doing business. After all, customers move, and there's nothing you can do about it, right?

Yes and No...

Yes, customers move. And there's nothing you can do about that.

But the usual rate of customer attrition is not just a fact of life. It's not just a cost of doing business.

The largest share of customer attrition is actually a cost of doing business poorly!

Here's an eye opener:

According to a recent study, if you run a typical business, here's a breakout of where your customer attrition is coming from.

We'll start with a group of one hundred customers who stopped patronizing you.

Four of them moved away. There's nothing you can do about them.

Fifteen of them developed another friend in the business or found someplace that has lower prices.

Another fifteen of them are not happy with the product they purchased from you and might be blaming you for it (as well as telling their friends that it's your fault).

Let's see now... $4 + 15 + 15 = 34$.

We've accounted for only thirty four out of a hundred people who are no longer doing business with you. And there's probably not too much you can do to salvage those thirty four people.

But what about the other sixty six people?

They didn't leave because of anything that you "*did.*"

They're not really angry or dissatisfied with you.

They left because they thought you didn't care about them.

You didn't make them feel special.

They felt that either you or one of your employees seemed to be indifferent about whether or not they did business with you.

But you don't *have* to lose these people (and the thousands of dollars in sales and referrals that they represent).

The solution is painfully simple.

Treat all of your customers like they're special.

Make sure that every employee in your company (even if they don't typically have much customer contact) knows that the customer is truly "*King*" or "*Queen.*"

Think about the TV show, "Cheers." The theme song says, "*Sometimes you want to be where everybody knows your name.*"

Have your employees learn and call your customers by their names whenever possible. That alone will keep many of them coming back.

Of course, that's just the basics.

Take it a step further.

What is it like (from the customer's view) to do business with your company?

Is it fun? (Like going to the circus)

And...

Is it easy? (Or must they jump through hoops.)

*Realizing his childhood dream, Bob discovers that
"running away to join the circus" isn't all it's cracked up to be.*

When it comes to your business, it's impossible to provide too much service...

It's impossible to make doing business with you too easy...

It's impossible to make doing business with you too convenient...

It's impossible for you to make doing business with you too much fun...

It's impossible to do too much for your customers...

But, you should always try!

If you promise (and deliver) benefits and advantages to the customer for doing business with you, you'll get the business. We covered that in the preceding *"secrets."*

But you want to go further... much further.

You want to make doing business with you entertaining.

You want customers to think of it as a good time.

You want them to look forward to it.

Not just the results of their transaction... Not just the benefits or advantages that they'll realize, but the actual process of doing business with you.

Start by looking at your business through your customer's eyes.

Here's a great story that illustrates how a typical customer can see your business differently than you do.

Neither of us can remember where we first heard it, so we can't credit the author, but it made such an impression on us that we both remembered the example.

It's the story of a small town candy store. This candy store is owned by a wonderful little old lady named Mrs. Sweettooth. (She needs a name, doesn't she?)

Mrs. Sweettooth not only loved her work, but she also loved the local children who would always crowd in after school to buy her treats.

Anyway, Mrs. Sweettooth employed two clerks, Betty and Mary, to serve customers at her huge candy counters.

One day, as the normal crowd of after school kids flooded her shop, Mrs. Sweettooth noticed that there were twice as many kids in the line waiting for Betty as there were waiting for Mary.

This puzzled her, but the candy timer went off calling her back to her candy making duties in the kitchen and she quickly forgot about the lines of children.

The next day, she again noticed that there were twice as many kids at Betty's counter as there were at Mary's.

And again, she thought this was peculiar.

So she went to the end of Betty's line and asked little Johnny why he was waiting in such a long line when Mary's line was so much shorter.

Johnny looked up and said: *"That's easy, Mrs. Sweettooth, Betty gives us more candy for our quarter."*

Well, Mrs. Sweettooth knew that she had to look into this. After all, even though she did love the kids, this is a business, and you can't simply give your products away.

Besides, at only 50 cents a pound (it was a long, long time ago), she was already selling her candy as cheaply as she could, and still stay in business.

She decided to keep a close watch on Betty.

The next day, when the usual crowd of kids came in, and the same lopsided situation with the lines developed, she watched Betty sell her candy.

Each time a child would put his or her quarter on the counter, Betty would sell them exactly half a pound of candy.

"Good," she thought. *"Betty is giving them a half pound of candy and charging for a half pound of candy."*

Her next reaction was, *"Oh my, that means that Mary must be short changing these wonderful children. That's even worse than giving them too much."*

She glanced over at Mary's counter, and saw that each time a child put a quarter on the counter, Mary would also carefully measure out a half pound of candy.

"Well, I don't understand this," she thought. *"Both Betty and Mary are giving the kids a half pound of candy for a quarter, but they all seem to think that Betty is giving them more."*

Finally, she decided to ask little Johnny exactly why he thought that Betty was giving the kids more candy for the same quarter.

The next day, as the kids were streaming in, Mrs. Sweettooth pulled Johnny aside, and gave him two quarters.

"Johnny, here's two quarters. I want you to buy a quarter's worth of candy from both Betty and Mary."

Johnny said, *"Sure, Mrs. Sweettooth, but you'll get more candy if you buy them both from Betty."*

She just smiled and said, *"That's OK, dear. Buy a quarter's worth from each of them."*

Well, when Johnny got to the front of Betty's line, she measured out exactly a half pound of candy and gave it to him for his quarter. And when he got to the front of Mary's line, she also gave him exactly a half pound of candy for his quarter.

Johnny brought the candy to Mrs. Sweettooth, and said, *"I told you to get all of your candy from Betty, she gives more candy for a quarter."*

Mrs. Sweettooth said, *"Johnny, what makes you feel that Betty gives more candy?"*

"It's simple, Mrs. Sweettooth, they both start with a big scoop of candy, but Betty keeps adding more, and Mary takes some away. So," he said triumphantly, *"you get more candy from Betty!"*

Mrs. Sweettooth glanced over at her counter girls, and sure enough, Mary would take a large scoop of candy and put it on the scale. Then she would slowly take some off, a little at a time until she had exactly half a pound of candy on the scale.

Betty, on the other hand would start with a little smaller scoop, and keep adding candy until she had exactly half a pound of candy on the scale.

"That's amazing," she thought. *"The kids sure picked up on something here."*

That evening, Mrs. Sweettooth asked both Betty and Mary about the way they sold candy.

Mary shrugged her shoulders and said that she just measured out the amount of candy that the customer wants and sells it to them with a smile.

Betty blushed a little, and said, "*I figure that people just want to get their money's worth, and nobody likes to see you take anything away from them. So, I simply make sure that I always start with less than what the customer orders, and then keep adding more until the scale reads the correct amount. That way, people seem to feel like they're getting something more. They seem to like that.*"

That evening, Mrs. Sweettooth had Betty teach Mary the *"right"* way to sell candy.

Make that the right way to sell anything!

Do you have Betty's and Mary's in your company?

Which do you think your customers prefer?

Remember, look at your own business even *more critically* than your *pickiest* customer.

What do you see?

If you have a retail store, is it clean?

Is it inviting? Does the general layout and display area reach out and encourage the customer to be part of it, or is it sterile?

Walk into your store and look at your employees. Are they smiling? Do they really look like they're enjoying themselves?

Are they genuinely pleased to help every customer? Do they sometimes seem to ignore the customers, or, at the other extreme, do they pounce on customers like animals looking for a fresh kill?

Are your salespeople more interested in making sales than creating lifelong customers?

The most powerful sales strategy in the world is not comprised of fancy closing techniques...

It's not made up of 101 great opening lines...

It doesn't consist of a group of fail-safe answers to customer objections...

The most successful salespeople in the world all have one thing in common...

The honest desire to serve their customers!

When you do that better than anyone else, the sales will take care of themselves.

Of course, your sales staff is only part of your customer service force.

What about the receptionist?

What happens when customers call on the phone?

Do your people answer the phone promptly? Cheerfully?

Are they truly helpful? Do they have the answers that your customers need?

These are just some of the obvious things that you must do to survive for the long term.

Think about how you can make doing business with you more convenient.

Make it easier. Make it totally *"hassle-free."*

We once saw a promotion from a florist that earned them a *"gold"* medal (in our eyes as well as their customers') for making it easy to do business with them.

They ran a special promotion that generated hundreds and hundreds of new customers who bought again and again. This one idea virtually catapulted them to the top of their market.

Here's what they did.

They knew that at certain times of the year, beautiful roses were so plentiful that they could buy them for pennies.

Well, the next time one of these *"glut"* periods came, they sent a letter to thousands of local business people and professionals.

The letter was sent to the recipient's office address.

The letter talked about how, in the hustle and bustle of everyday life, it's not unusual to sometimes forget to tell "that someone special" in our lives how much we really appreciate them.

It acknowledged how busy the recipient usually is and that sometimes it's hard to remember those important dates when flowers would be an appropriate gift to these important people in their lives.

And, the letter went on to make the following offer...

We'd like to buy you a dozen beautiful long stem roses to send to that "*someone special*" today... In fact, simply fill out and return the enclosed card, and we'll rush these gorgeous roses to whom ever you indicate, the same day we receive it.

And we'll do it absolutely free!

We're doing this for two reasons.

First, we want you (and your "*someone special*") to see for yourselves the beautiful flowers and expert service that we always provide.

And secondly, we want to introduce you to our new "*Special V.I.P. Customer Program.*"

Simply fill out the enclosed card showing the names, addresses, birthdays, anniversaries, and any other special dates that might be an appropriate time to send flowers. Don't forget your spouse, girlfriend (or boyfriend), mother, grandmother, in-laws, aunts, secretary, etc.

We'll keep it on file and give you a phone call a few days prior to these important dates.

If you'd like to send flowers when we call, great. We'll take care of everything and mail you an invoice a few days later. As a "*Special V.I.P. Customer,*" you even get thirty day payment terms.

If you've made other arrangements and decide not to send flowers on that date, that's OK, too, because you're under no obligation, and we'll never nag you.

But honestly now, even if you don't want to send flowers, wouldn't it be nice to get a friendly little confidential reminder of those important dates.

Think of us as your own little *"special dates reminder secretary."*

Remember, there's never any obligation to send flowers, but we're there for you when you need us.

Wow! Who could refuse an offer like that?

As you can imagine, we signed up in a flash.

And just like they promised, they called us a few days before each of those important dates.

And as you can probably imagine, often we'd forgotten an upcoming birthday or anniversary.

And as you can guess, we usually decided to send flowers. After all, how much easier could it be? We were already on the phone with the florist. All we had to do was tell them what to say on the card. They already had the correct names and addresses.

Believe us, that florist made back many, many times the cost of that free dozen roses.

And when other times came up that we needed to send flowers, for sick friends, customers, or anything else, who do you think we called?

That's right.

Never underestimate the value of making it easy and convenient for your customers to do business with you.

The easier you make it, the more money you'll make. It's that simple.

What's that?

You want to make even more money?

OK. Well, instead of just making it easy for your customers to do business with you...

Make it FUN for them
to do business with you.

Look around, you'll see some examples of this.

In fact, you don't have to look any further than your local McDonald's.

Most of them have now installed a full-scale playground for their younger customers. They've spent a fortune on these play areas. The kids can play in them for free.

They know that the more fun they make it for the kids, the more often the kids are going to beg (nag) mom and dad to bring them to McDonald's.

This means more bottom line profits. Far more than the one time cost of installing a playground.

Another example from McDonald's is the *"Happy Meal."*

Frankly, our kids don't even care that much for the food, but they've simply got to get the new toy for the week that comes free with every *"Happy Meal."*

And get this, the silly little toy probably costs McDonald's no more than a few cents.

But those toys sell hundreds of thousands of *"Happy Meals."*

Here's an example from our old video stores...

One day we came up with the idea of selling popcorn in our stores. We figured that nothing goes better with movies than popcorn, so we looked into getting some popcorn machines like they use in movie theaters.

Well, when we realized how inexpensive the machines were, and how down right cheap popcorn was (we paid about $6.50 each for fifty pound cases), we decided to offer it free to all of our customers.

Just the smell of fresh hot popped popcorn in our stores added to the theater atmosphere. It made it more fun to stop by and pick up some movies.

But we went even one step further...

We were a large advertiser, so we went to the local Coca Cola distributer and asked them to provide us with free soft drinks for our customers.

We pointed out that they were always spending a fortune promoting one or another of their products. Sometimes it was Diet Coke, sometimes New Coke, sometimes Coke Classic, etc.

We told them that if they would supply soft drink fountains for our stores (dispensing whichever product they were pushing at the time), we'd promote their products in all of our advertising.

Our customers loved it. They got free popcorn, and some great soft drinks to wash it down.

They came to our stores more often and stayed longer. Therefore, they always found some movies to rent making it exceedingly profitable for us.

But the best example of *"making doing business with you fun"* that we've ever seen is a laundromat.

What could be harder to make fun
than a trip to the laundromat?

Like any laundromat, they had dozens of coin-operated washing machines and dryers.

But that's where the similarities ended!

Naturally, they made *"laundry day"* more convenient for their customers.

They had not one or two, but three or more attendants on duty all of the time. Of course, with the crowds that they attracted, they needed all of that help.

All of their machines were kept squeaky-clean. In fact, they had an attendant clean the machines after every use.

And they always had plenty of every kind of laundry product imaginable (including some ecologically sound ones).

And they even sold hangers for people who didn't bring enough.

They certainly reduced the hassle of *"laundry day,"* but that's not enough to make doing your laundry fun, is it?

Well, this place did something more.

They recognized that most of the people that use a laundromat are young adults, and that many of them were single.

And what they did next is so novel, so unique, and so brilliant, that it's possibly the best example of common sense business in the world.

They turned the laundromat into a party place!

They started by dressing up the place to look more like a neighborhood "watering hole," than a laundromat.

Then they put in a snack bar and a beer tap, and they provided music, and TV's (with cable).

In fact, they even put in some pool tables, video games, and darts.

And they turned their laundromat into one of the hottest party places in town.

It became a great place to meet people, and the more popular it became, the hotter it got.

Soon, it was the place to be... even if you didn't have laundry to do.

And they profited handsomely from it.

All because they made doing
laundry easy, fun, and exciting.

Of course, you don't have to invent a whole new business concept to make doing business with you more fun or convenient or just plain easier.

There are dozens and dozens of things that you can do to make your customers love you.

Think about any little extra touches that you can have your staff provide. These little things cost next to nothing, but they really stick out in your customer's mind.

Remember when we talked about S.O.B.'s? We looked at a few ways that grocery stores could really set themselves apart. Some of those things really increase the level of customer service to superstar levels.

For example: A grocery store should make it a policy that anytime a customer asked an employee where to find a particular item, that employee (no matter what their "*job description*") should take the customer right to the item, rather than just point and tell them what aisle to look at.

In fact, they should go one step further. The employee should then ask, "*May I help you find anything else on your shopping list? It might save you some time.*"

Imagine the impact on the customer.

Suppose you had a home improvement store or lumberyard.

You should make certain that you always have enough help on duty to make sure that the customer never has to help load his purchase into (or onto) his vehicle.

In fact, you should consider fast, free delivery. That would make it much easier for the customer, wouldn't it?

Also, if you've ever bought lumber for a home project, you've probably noticed that some of the boards on the stack are kind of crooked, split, or knotty, while some of them are perfect; even though they're all supposed to be of the same general grade.

A smart lumber company would separate them and only sell the perfect ones for full price, and should offer the less than perfect ones for a discount.

Many lumberyards won't cut any wood for customers. Most of the ones that do, charge a ridiculous fee for this service. Imagine how much a beginning home handyman would appreciate getting his wood cut to size for free.

Suppose the lumberyard always had a *"handyman-expert"* on duty. They could promote free expert advice for any project. Chances are that the *"handyman-expert"* could show most of the customers how to save money on their projects.

Sure, this might cost a few dollars in sales *today*, but the increased *repeat sales* from happy customers would, by far, make up for that.

Here's another way to use a combination of educating your customers and great customer service that could pay huge dividends.

Hold FREE home improvement classes in the evenings and on weekends. Teach your customers how to do more home projects, and they'll surely buy more supplies and even tools from you.

Video tape these classes and sell them to your customers, or even better, let your customers borrow any tape from the library for FREE.

The key is look to the obvious... and beyond.

Here's another one of our favorites.

A restaurant that we frequent has one of their waiters or waitresses circulate around the dining room with samples of some of their best dishes.

They offer all of the patrons the chance to taste any of these dishes before they decide on their order. The taste is FREE. Of course, they decide what to feature for the taste test based on what is profitable to sell, or what they may have too much of.

But when they do this, two things happen.

One is that they significantly increase sales of what they want to sell...

The other is that the customers absolutely love this sneak

preview. It not only makes them feel special, it also practically eliminates the chance of them being less than thrilled with what they order.

It makes the dining experience virtually guaranteed. And that guarantees that the customer will come back again and again.

Another restaurant that we know has a special service for rainy days.

They have several people who meet you in the parking lot when you arrive. These people escort you into the restaurant under an umbrella.

When you are finished with your meal, and are ready to leave, they escort you back to your car; again under the colorful umbrella.

But get this...

After they get you into your car, safe, sound and dry, they take out another umbrella (naturally, with the restaurant's logo on it), and hand it to you.

They tell you how much they really appreciate the fact that you braved the lousy weather just to come dine with them, and they'd like you to keep the umbrella as a thank you gift.

So you see, the real key to massive profits is simple...

Make your company more convenient, more fun, more service oriented, more exciting than any other, and you'll profit immensely.

Now let's turn to the next "*Gold-Mine Secret*" and see if we can compound these profits even more...

The After Dinner Mint!

In this, the second of the "*Gold-Mine Secrets,*" we're going to talk about what happens *after* your customer makes a purchase.

You've finally set the stage to start cashing in on those huge gold nuggets that we've helped you find. By now, you should be thinking of each one of your customers as a perpetual source of those "*gold nuggets.*"

In most businesses, it costs many times more to develop a new customer than it does to maintain and nurture an existing one.

But for some strange reason, many companies that spend a fortune on marketing to get those new customers don't spend a dime (or even a moment's worth of effort) to keep them.

What a wasteful folly.

Suppose you spend $1,000 in advertising and this advertising brings in 50 new customers.

That means that each customer represents a marketing investment of $20.

Of course, *your* numbers could be quite different. Perhaps you'll find that it costs you as little as $5 in marketing per new customer, or as much as a few hundred dollars.

It doesn't really matter, as long as your profit margin from your total sales covers it (as well as your other overhead).

The point is, that regardless of how much, it costs you a fairly significant amount of money to find a prospect and develop him into a customer for the first time.

In fact, the cost of acquiring this new customer is usually between five and 100 times the cost of keeping him happy. And a happy customer will buy from you again and again.

We already discussed one way to make your customers happy in the previous *"secret."*

Namely... *"Service them to high heaven."*

Amaze them with levels of customer service unlike anything they've ever before seen, and they'll be yours for life.

But so far, we've mainly addressed what you should do before and during the time that the customer is in the actual process of doing business with you.

Now what should you do *after* the customer buys?

Sometimes it's just the little things that make a <u>good</u> place <u>GREAT</u>!

Well, when you go to a fine restaurant, what happens after you finish your meal and settle the bill?

They give you an after dinner mint, right?

Well, that's exactly what you should do for your customers.

No, not literally, but in a manner of speaking. The point is the same.

You must make absolutely certain that, after they've made their purchase, they still have "*a pleasant taste in their mouths.*"

How do you do this?

Call, write, or visit your customer
within the first 24 hours of their purchase.

It's not a social call, and believe it or not, it's not a sales call either...

It's a "*post-purchase reassurance call*"
that could provide you with an annuity that
will pay you dividends for years to come!

Let's look at what is happening in most customers' minds before, during, and immediately after they make a purchase.

In the very beginning (the educational and early selling phases), most prospects are mildly interested, somewhat disinterested, or even downright skeptical of you and your product or service.

But through great marketing (as a result of reading this book, we hope) you do manage to get their attention.

You educate them in a very nonthreatening way. You explain why and how your product or service will solve some problem in the prospect's life or provide some important advantage or benefit to them.

By now, the prospects are definitely interested. In fact, they've decided to call, write, or come in to find out more. With the correct sales presentation (either in person or by phone or mail) they're ready to buy.

You dazzle them with an amazing amount of attention and service.

You show them beyond any doubt that you are the kind of company that they want to do business with, and top it off by making them an incredible deal. (An *"incredible deal"* does not necessarily mean the lowest price. It's the *highest perceived value for the price.*)

Congratulations. You did everything right and you made the sale.

Right now the customer is happy...

...happy about making the purchase.

...happy with you and your company.

...happy about solving his or her problem.

...happy about all of the added benefits and advantages that you told them to expect.

Basically they're just plain happy!

But this happy, euphoric state of mind doesn't last long.

A funny thing happens in the time span between the customer making the purchase and when he or she first starts using the product or service.

Some people call this phenomenon *"Buyer's Remorse"*...

Others call it *"Post-Purchase Dissonance"*...

Here's what happens. Little *"doubt gremlins"* invade your customer's mind and play havoc with those good feelings that you worked so hard to cultivate.

These evil little creatures disrupt the normal, rational thought process of customers and put them through an emotional ringer with thoughts like...

"Oh no, I let that salesman talk me into this."

Or, *"What if I bought the wrong model?"*

Or, *"I don't know if that salesman was telling the truth, or just saying what he thought I wanted to hear."*

Or, *"I probably paid way too much; I should have shopped around more."*

Or, *"Do I even really need this thing?"*

Or, *"There are dozens of other, more important things that I should have done with my money."*

Or, *"How am I going to pay for this?"*

Or, *"What am I going to tell my wife/husband?"*

Or anything else that makes the customer question whether or not it was a wise decision to do business with you.

If you leave the customers to their own devices (these little *"doubt gremlins"*), they'll quickly talk themselves out of being happy with you and your products.

In fact, some of them will decide that you used some kind of voodoo or black magic to unfairly and unethically influence them to buy.

Even though you didn't, these people will make themselves unhappy and blame you for it.

They'll become a costly (and unnecessary), source of refunds, exchanges, and phantom complaints.

Although most of them don't become actively disgruntled, many will still have doubts and insecurities about their decision to buy. When it comes to the actual product or service, they may not even give it a fair try.

They'll already be biased against it.

Even in the best of circumstances; even when the customer manages to ward off the majority of those doubts, they'll still lose that good feeling they had about you and your product.

A feeling that you worked hard to develop.

At best, you're back to ground zero with these people.

But it doesn't have to be that way.

A good *"Post-Purchase Reassurance Call,"* (or after dinner mint) will not only keep you in their good graces, but, when done properly, can even elevate you beyond the level of good feeling that they had at the time of purchase.

**Just look at some of the things that this
simple phone call, letter, or visit can do for you.**

It can prove to the customer that the terrific customer service that he or she experienced at the time of purchase was honest and *"for real."*

It can prove that your service wasn't just a fluke. And it wasn't just a ploy to make the sale.

It gives you a chance to resell the product or service and reinforce what a shrewd purchase the customer made.

It can give you a chance to reduce or even eliminate costly exchanges or refunds.

It can give you a chance to further endear the customer to you which will make additional, future sales much easier.

It can give you a chance to explain additional uses of the product or service so the customer will get more use out of it (as well as reorder sooner).

All of these things are like *"money in the bank."*

That's quite a powerful little marketing step, isn't it?

Here's an example of the simplest form of post-purchase reassurance letter.

A simple Thank You note.

Dear Mr. Smith,

I just wanted to drop you a note to again thank you for your patronage.

You know, all too often, the people we do business with tend to focus on "getting the sale," and then forgetting the customer by the time he gets out the door.

That's certainly not the case here at Widget World.

We truly do value and appreciate your patronage, and look forward to serving you again.

Again, thanks for you confidence in us. We'll work hard to continue to earn it.

Warmly,

H. Brad Antin

Widget Consultant

P.S. If you have any questions about your new widget, please give me a call at 555-1234. I'll be happy to answer them.

That simple little thank you note will help build an ongoing relationship with your new customer.

After all, even that most basic form of customer recognition is sadly missing from most businesses today.

The mere fact that you acknowledged the customer and thanked him or her after the sale, conveys a certain amount of reassurance that they made the right choice.

But why not go one step further...

Why not get the customer back to the frame of mind he or she was in when they made the purchase?

Why not actually resell them on the product, as well as yourself?

Why not try to eliminate any of those lingering fears that the customer might be feeling about their decision?

Try a more detailed letter in which you remind the customer of some of the important benefits and advantages that they can now enjoy.

Reinforce the high level of service that the customer experienced at the time of sale, and the feeling that this extraordinary service will continue into the future.

And give the customer the tools to justify that buying decision to any and all doubters.

Basically, this kind of post-purchase reassurance letter or call is not fundamentally different from a good sales presentation. In fact, the only difference is that you're not trying to sell them anything new.

Instead, you're merely reselling what they've already bought. This is usually much easier because you're not asking them for anymore money. They don't see any ulterior motive, and they are more likely to believe you.

And just like when you sold them the first time, and showed them all of the benefits that your product will provide them, you have to appeal to their emotions.

That's where most people make the buying decision. Of course, you must also give them the logical, rational reasons for buying. That's how they justify their purchase decision to themselves as well as their friends, spouses, co-workers, boss, etc.

The point is quite simple, really.

All you need to do is rekindle that warm happy feeling that they had at the time of purchase.

Prove to them again, what a great decision it was, and you'll develop a customer for life.

Here's a simple example...

Dear Mr. Smith,

I'm writing this note to you for two reasons, really.

First, to again thank you for your business. I want you to know that we really do appreciate your support, and we'll bend over backwards to continue to give you the kind of exceptional service that you deserve.

In fact, that's exactly what we've become known for -- exceptional customer service.

Secondly, I wanted to make sure that you're enjoying your new widget, and remind you of a few important facts about your new widget.

I don't know if you remember this, but your model xyz widget is capable of storing up to 12 different pre-programmed routines.

The programming commands are listed on page 6 of your owners manual. These pre-programmed routines will allow you to enjoy your widget a lot more than most standard widgets, and you'll probably be the envy of every widget owning friend you have.

Another valuable feature of your new widget is the automatic stand by mode. This allows you to leave your widget on 24 hours a day. The stand by mode uses only about one dollar's worth of electricity per month, and keeps your widget ready for use whenever you need it. You can forget all of the lengthy warm up procedures that other widgets require.

By the way, if you have any problems or questions at all concerning your widget, please give me a call at the store. My direct number is 555-1234.

Chances are I'll be able to talk you through the procedure right on the phone and save you a lot of time and effort. I'd be really happy to help, so don't hesitate to call.

Oh yes, I happened to run across an interesting fact about the xyz widget. The latest survey of users of all brands of widgets shows that this model of widget has the lowest operating cost of any widget available. In fact, it costs only 75 cents per day to operate, and that's including supplies and electricity.

Well, thanks again for shopping with us, and if there is ever anything we can do to help you in the future, please don't hesitate to call.

We are truly here to serve you.

Warmly,

Alan J. Antin

Do you see how much more a simple letter like this accomplishes than just a thank you note?

Now, the customer is resold on *both* the product and you. The customer can start to believe that all of those wonderful things that you promised will indeed come true.

The post-purchase reassurance letter takes on an even greater importance when you've sold the product by mail.

Typically, there is a much longer time frame between when the customer orders the product and when he or she receives it.

In this case, you should send a post-purchase reassurance letter to the customer (via first class mail) the same day that you get the order.

That's right, the same day.

In case you're wondering why you should send a post-purchase reassurance letter before the customer even receives the product, consider this...

In a retail sale, the customer typically gets the product at the time of sale. He or she can start enjoying the benefits of their purchase immediately.

Just using the product can help allay some of those post-purchase fears and doubts.

But in the case of mail order, the customer will start experiencing those fears and doubts *before* they receive the product.

You've got nothing on your side to combat these doubts, so they can very easily undermine the sale.

But if you immediately send a wonderful post-purchase reassurance letter detailing what an intelligent buying decision the customer has made, you'll have better than a fighting chance of keeping the sale.

This letter should resell the product or service and help them justify the purchase with even more facts, figures, testimonials, and reasons why they made this great decision in the first place.

Another great tool to use in this case is an *"unexpected bonus."*

In your post-purchase reassurance letter, tell them about some extra, unexpected bonus that you are going to send them along with what they've ordered.

But don't tell them all about the bonus, just enough to get them excited and curious. This will give them another reason to eagerly await their purchase.

Think of the affect this could have on C.O.D. Sales!

If you've decided not to sell anything by C.O.D. because of the cost of customer refusals, you might want to rethink your position.

If you had a way of getting more people to accept delivery, those extra sales could add up to a tidy profit, couldn't they?

Well, this technique could be exactly what you need.

In fact, just telling them to look for this extra little surprise could cut your delivery refusals by half or even more. Try it.

Let's look at a couple of real life examples of how some companies use unexpected bonuses in their post-purchase reassurance programs to make a big impression on their customers...

A friend of ours bought a new Mercedes Benz last year.

He was quite impressed with the level of service and attention he received from the dealer leading up to the sale, even though he was looking at one of the smaller (less expensive) models which they offer.

Of course, you'd expect a high degree of attention when you are considering the purchase of a luxury car like a Mercedes (no matter what model you choose).

Anyway, here's what happened after he bought the car...

A few days after our friend got his new car, he received a complete package of information about the unique and comprehensive roadside assistance program that the dealer (and Mercedes) had set up for him.

The package described the benefits of this program in detail.

It included a special T.L.C. (Tender Loving Care) Card that included a nationwide "800" number that my friend could call if he ever had a problem with his car while traveling anywhere in the United States.

The letter explained that with this card, all our friend had to do was make a simple toll free phone call, and the nearest Mercedes dealer would immediately dispatch a roadside assistance car to him.

If the roadside assistance technician could solve the problem on the spot, he would; if not, he would tow the car into the shop for immediate repairs.

It told how this dealer would repair his car at no charge and get him back on the road in the least amount of time possible.

It told him that if, for some reason, the dealer needed to keep his car overnight, Mercedes would pay for his hotel room, meals and any other incidental expenses that came up.

And it explained the extraordinary measures they would go through to make sure that should he ever need assistance, they would provide it with the minimum amount of inconvenience to him.

The letter also mentioned that most Mercedes owners experience a high level of pride of ownership and like to keep their cars clean.

It went on to say that our friend could bring his car in every Saturday for a free car wash and wax (including the complete interior).

That's a pretty good post-purchase reassurance program in itself, but that's not all our friend's Mercedes dealer did.

A couple of weeks later, our friend received a big package from his Mercedes dealer.

This package had a card that was hand-written by the salesman who had sold our friend the car. The card said how much the salesman appreciated the business, and that he was confident that our friend was enjoying the prestige and comfort of driving such a fine car.

The package contained a picnic basket that included a fine bottle of wine, two crystal wine glasses, and a wonderful assortment of fruits, nuts, crackers, and cheeses. The salesman suggested that our friend and his wife (he mentioned her by name), take the picnic basket and go for a nice drive to the beach, and have a quiet, romantic little picnic with his compliments.

Next, about 30 days after my friend had purchased the car, he got a phone call from the salesman. The salesman again expressed his appreciation for the sale, and said he just wanted to make sure that everything was going well, and that our friend was happy.

Next, our friend had to bring the car in for it's 1,200 mile check. This was, of course, provided free by the dealership. He was given an appointment at his convenience, and when he arrived for this appointment, he was greeted by name.

Our friend was shown into a very comfortable waiting room, offered coffee, snacks, and a newspaper, or magazine.

Just about the time he finished reading the paper, he was told that his car was ready.

When he got into his car, he noticed that they had not only performed the needed maintenance, but they had also washed and waxed his car.

Two days later, our friend got a call from the service manager of the dealership.

The service manager wanted to make sure that everything was done satisfactorily, and asked about every aspect of the service appointment.

He wanted to be sure that our friend was treated well in the waiting room, that he'd had anything he could want while waiting, that his car was returned cleaned and waxed, and even that the seats and mirrors were in the same positions that our friend had left them in.

But, believe it or not, the dealership still wasn't finished pampering our friend...

A few months later, on our friend's birthday, he received another picnic basket with a bottle of fine wine, two crystal goblets, fancy fruits, nuts, and cheeses, and a birthday card.

And then on the birthday of our friend's wife, another picnic basket and birthday card arrived.

And, believe it or not, on Christmas, our friend received another picnic basket and card.

Can you imagine how these well-timed gifts made our friend feel? Where do you think he'll buy his next car?

Of course, this is an extreme example of post-purchase reassurance, but it teaches an important point.

Sure, the Mercedes dealer spent a fortune on our friend; perhaps as much as a few hundred dollars. But compared with the thousands of dollars that they'll make if they sell him another car, it's a drop in the bucket.

Suppose you don't sell extremely expensive cars, what could you do to impress your customers?

Maybe you sell giant screen televisions.

If that were the case, you might want to have your salespeople find out what kinds of televised events their customers most enjoy.

Perhaps, if the customers are particularly interested in sports, you could send them a great post-purchase reassurance letter and tell them that you'd like to help them throw a little sports party. They could invite their friends to come over and watch the big game on their new giant screen.

You could put together a deal with a local deli or grocery store to buy party platters for a discount (based on your anticipated volume).

Include a certificate for a wonderful platter along with preprinted invitations, and other party necessities.

Or, if you sold pools and spas, you could do the same thing for a pool or hot tub party.

Use your imagination. You'll come up with all kinds of things that you could include in your post-purchase reassurance efforts.

One more quick little example, and then we'll move on.

A travel agent with whom we did business had a great post-purchase reassurance technique.

After you booked a vacation trip through them, they would send you a series of books and magazines that told all about your destination.

These weren't just travel brochures, mind you. They were beautiful hard-cover books that told everything there was to know about your destination.

They told of local customs, history, what to see and do, and how to enjoy your destination with the knowledge of an insider.

The travel agent sent a new book or magazine about every week or two, and by the time you went on your trip, you were as well versed on the location as a world traveler.

It was a nice touch. And it kept your level of excitement and anticipation of your trip peaked right up to departure day.

OK, so now you've designed and implemented a great customer post purchase reassurance program, and your customers all have "*a good taste in their mouths.*"

It's time to start mining those "*gold nuggets.*"

One way is to follow your first post-purchase reassurance effort with another one.

That's right, a week or so following your first post-purchase reassurance effort, you should contact the customer again.

Again thank the customer for his or her business. Ask if there's anything you can do for them, or if they have any further questions.

Make them feel good again, and then ask them if they had some friends or associates who would appreciate the same kind of service and value that they've received from you.

Explain that you'd really appreciate any referrals that they could steer your way, and that you promise to treat their friends with a special touch.

You'll be surprised at how many people will gladly refer their friends to you.

But that's only the beginning...

The final "*Gold-Mine Secret*" deals with developing, cultivating, and mining what will probably become the biggest source of profits your company has ever seen.

Let's turn now and see why "*You Can't Move Forward Without Your Back-End.*"

The Twelfth Secret:

You Can't Move Forward
Without Your Back-End!

Well, we hope you've paid close attention to the last two *"Gold-Mine Secrets,"* because now we're going to show you how to use them to find a virtual *"pot of gold."*

If you stopped reading this book right now (although we can't imagine why you'd want to), and merely applied what you've already learned, you'd be quite successful at finding and mining *"gold nuggets"* by the hundreds.

But we promised to teach you more than that.

We promised that we weren't going to merely preach that you should take good care of your customers.

We promised that by showing you a dimension of customer service that went far beyond the obvious, you would profit handsomely.

Well, here's the payoff... *"The Pot Of Gold."*

In this *"secret,"* we're going to show you how to transform those good feelings which you worked hard to cultivate, into an enormous flood of new (and ongoing) profits.

These are profits that hardly cost you anything to generate and will see you through even the most dismal of economic conditions.

But, frankly, if you don't follow through on everything we taught you in the last two *"secrets,"* the windfall profits that we're going to talk about now will not materialize.

In fact, you should probably stop and go back and reread those two sections right now.

The key to those two "*secrets*" is to simply...

Do the right thing!

Provide an amazing amount of customer service and your customers will support you again and again.

The first time you got them to buy, you had to overcome a certain level of distrust. Remember, they perceived all of the risk of doing business with you as resting squarely on *their* shoulders.

But you reassured them, and they decided to give you one chance. Then, you amazed them with an unprecedented level of customer service, and built up a level of trust and credibility in their minds that will now bring you huge rewards.

If you really did it right, *you own them.* They are your customers, and your competitors have almost no chance of stealing them away.

Here's a quick (but quite common) example of how great customer service really does pay off.

Back when we were in the video business, Alan happened to help a Chinese couple who came into one of our stores.

The husband spoke almost no English at all, and the wife spoke just barely enough to get by.

They owned a successful Chinese restaurant in town, and since business was good, they had decided to get themselves a little treat.

They wanted to buy a giant screen TV for their new home.

When they came in, though, they had a chip on their shoulders the size of a redwood tree. They didn't believe a word that Alan was saying, and they seemed sure that they were going be taken advantage of.

We later found out that they generally received extremely poor service no matter where they shopped.

This was probably because they were visibly different (first generation Chinese immigrants), and they were very difficult to communicate with because of their poor English.

It seems that many of the salespeople that they came across tried to take advantage of them by trying to sell them junk, or trying to "*high gross*" them by jacking up the price.

Perhaps these unprofessional (and foolish) salespeople figured that since they couldn't speak English very well, they were some how not as smart as other people. How ridiculous.

Other salespeople simply wouldn't take the time or effort to work with them. They merely brushed them off. Again, how ridiculous.

Anyway, when they shopped at our store, Alan patiently and carefully explained everything he could about our company and the various models of giant screens that we carried.

He told them about our terrific service department.

He told them about our customer service and follow up.

He told them about how our trained staff of installation experts would deliver and set up their giant screen.

And he spent plenty of time with them to make sure they understood everything.

They were very concerned about getting a brand new giant screen rather than one that had been on our sales floor. Of course, Alan assured them that they would get a brand new TV, still in its factory sealed box.

Well, finally they decided to buy their giant screen from Alan. Not because of the great reputation of our company, and not because of our service.

They didn't seem to believe a word of it anyway.

They bought from Alan because he at least took the time to listen to them, find out what they really wanted, and help them make the right choice.

Well, guess what happened next.

One by one, all of the promises that Alan had made started to come true.

On the morning of the day we were supposed to deliver their giant screen, our delivery manager called them and confirmed the directions to their home, and reminded them to expect our crew at around 1:00 that afternoon.

Sure enough, at 1:00 they saw our truck pull into their driveway.

Our deliver guys then proceeded to unload a brand new giant screen (still in it's factory sealed box), and asked where the customers would like it set up.

They put special packing blankets around the TV, and very carefully moved it into position.

They set up the giant screen and fine tuned all of the adjustments, and even took the *extra* time to explain every knob, button, and control to the customers.

They showed the customers how to clean the special screen, and they also went over the entire cabinet with furniture polish.

They carefully moved back into place any furniture that they had moved to set up the giant screen.

And they hauled away every piece of packing material and trash from the box away for the customers.

In short, they impressed the customers beyond measure that our company really cared about them.

The next day, the customers received a very nice post-purchase reassurance letter that was hand signed by Alan Antin, the President of the company.

A few days later the customers had a few questions about the TV and they dropped by the office to see Alan.

To their surprise, Alan dropped whatever he was doing and took care of them right away.

By now, they were "*true believers.*"

They now believed what Alan had tried to tell them about our customer service in the first place.

To say that these were now happy customers would be like calling The Grand Canyon a ditch. They were thrilled with us.

All because we treated them with caring respect, told the truth, and gave them great service.

Now, for the big pay off.

A few weeks later, they came into the office with a package almost as big as the box their giant screen came in.

Remember, they had a Chinese restaurant, and as a simple little "*thank you,*" they brought in enough food to feed our entire staff lunch for a week.

What's that? You want a more tangible pay off? You want to see results of a more financial nature?

Well, try this on for size...

Kansas City had a fairly large Chinese population, and these new customers of ours were highly regarded (and quite influential) in that community.

It turns out that this couple and their family were consumer electronics buffs.

Over the next couple of years, they made purchases from us that totaled somewhere in the neighborhood of $20,000.

But that's not all.

Whenever one of their friends wanted to buy a piece of electronics, they would not just recommend us, they would actually bring their friend in, and even interpret for them if necessary. These referrals brought in another $100,000 of sales.

Of course, we always gave them a good deal, but they were more than willing to let us make a reasonable profit. And they never questioned the price because they knew that we would always treat them more than just fairly.

They would usually just call or stop in and tell us the type of gadget they wanted next, and buy whichever one we suggested.

And we never let them down.

Sure, we could have taken advantage of the situation and built some extra profit in the deal. Or we could have used them to move something out of inventory that wasn't selling well. But we didn't.

We knew that as long as we took great care of our customers, they would come back time after time.

And that's where the real profits come from.

To see how big an impact this will have on your business, start with... The concept of *"the lifetime value of a customer"* (or *"the marginal net worth (to you) of a customer"*).

This will illustrate to you, the actual, dollars-and-cents logic of following our advice.

We're going to use a dry cleaner for this example, but you should use the same procedure for your business. Just plug in your own numbers.

First, answer these questions about your business.

1. How much is the average sale?

2. How many times per year does the average customer buy?

3. How many years will the average customer continue to buy (assuming you keep him or her happy)?

4. How many people will the average customer tell about your business?

5. What percentage of those referrals will become customers?

Remember, some customers are probably doing business with you only once, while others may be doing business with you several times a month or week.

Use an estimated average!

For our mythical dry cleaner, the numbers look like this...

A.	Average Sale	$15
B.	Number of Sales per year (2/mo)	24
C.	Number of years customer buys	4
D.	Number of referrals from customer	5
E.	% of referrals that become customers	25%
F.	Gross Sales per year (A x B)	$360
G.	Gross sales over life of customer (F x C)	$1,440
H.	Number of referrals that become customers (D x F)	1.25
I.	Gross Sales for total referrals (G x H)	$1,800
J.	Total Value of satisfied customer (G + I)	$3,240

What an eye-opener!

That $15 customer is actually worth $3,240 in sales to our dry cleaner which translates to about $1,000 in net, bottom line profit!

But hang on a minute...

Now that you know what a happy customer is worth, take a look at what an *unhappy* customer costs you.

I hope you're sitting down, because this might be a little bit shocking.

A.	Value of a satisfied customer	$3,240
B.	Studies show that a dissatisfied customer tells an average of 12 people	12
C.	% of those negative referrals that don't become customers because of it	25%
D.	Lost customers because of negative referrals (B x C)	3
E.	Value of lost customers as a result of negative referrals (A x D)	$9,720
F.	Total cost of one unhappy customer (A + E)	$12,960

Run this same exercise on your own company. The numbers will probably be even more dramatic!

By the way, the numbers used for the assumptions in this example were actually quite conservative.

Many times a happy customer will tell *more* than 5 people about you.

Many times a happy customer will influence *more* than 1.25 other people to actually become customers.

Many times an unhappy customer can cause *far more* than just 3 people to decide not to do business with you.

So you see, even though these numbers might sound somewhat fantastic, at first, they are probably still an understatement of how critical it is to have the very best customer service possible.

The best way to impress your employees with the importance of taking care of your customers is to sit down *with* them and figure out what each of those customers is really worth.

Don't keep this a secret from your employees, make sure they know it, and know it well.

In fact, you should probably train your staff to picture that $15 per time customer with a great big price tag on his chest.

Sure, the customer is only spending $15 *today*, but your employees should picture him wearing a $3,240 price tag! After all, that's what he's really worth to you.

All of these sales are based on doing nothing more than pleasing your customers.

And you didn't spend a dime or a moment's thought (other than developing a good customer service program), to get all of that repeat business.

Now you are ready to learn how to take this to the next level; a level of marketing and business savvy that will catapult you so far above your competitors that they'll never know what hit them...

We've spent the first part of this section trying to solidify and hammer home the importance of the last two "*secrets.*"

We've given examples and even showed you how to use the numbers from your own business to verify, in the most graphic way possible, the importance of these concepts.

It may seem to you that we've been redundant.

We have been!

We've done everything we could to make absolutely certain that you understand (and start to practice) these concepts.

Now let's move on to "*the pot of gold.*"

Your back-end *is* your "*pot of gold!*"

Let's start with a couple of definitions.

When you advertise your product or services and your advertising attracts a new customer, and that customer makes an initial purchase... That's your front-end.

Your front-end is the first sale
that you get from a new customer.

All other sales that you make to an existing customer make up your back-end.

Your back-end is the total of the
additional sales you get from a customer.

Ooops, there we go, being redundant again.

Remember our mythical dry cleaner?

In that case, the front end was $15 (the customer's initial purchase).

The back-end was $3,225 (all of the *additional* purchases from that customer and his referrals).

The dry cleaner was a good example, because the back-end is pretty much automatic. In other words, if all we did was take good care of our customers, they would come back again and again.

But, so far, the dry cleaner in our example had not *actively* worked the back-end.

And *your* business may or may not have as good an automatic back-end as a dry cleaner.

In fact, you may not even have a back-end at all, *yet*. But don't worry, because that's exactly what we're going to talk about for the rest of this "*secret*"...

How to develop and work your back-end!

Here's where the rubber meets the road.

First, look closely at your business.

Do you sell many different products or services that would or could be made attractive to the same customers?

Do you sell accessories, add-ons, or consumables that go with your products?

Do you sell repair or maintenance services for your products?

Do you sell a service that your customers should or could use more than once?

If you answered "yes" to any of these questions, your business already has great back-end potential.

But what if you couldn't answer "yes" to any of these questions? Does that mean that you can't go for the "*pot of gold*"?

Absolutely not!

Simply look for it somewhere else. Consider these questions.

Do you sell a product that is different than, but appeals to the same customers, as a friend's product?

Do you frequently get prospects who don't buy your product or service because they want or prefer a cheaper (or more expensive) version of what you sell?

Do you sell a product or service to customers who share a common need (other than your own products or services)?

Presto! You've got *great* back-end potential.

In short, almost every business has the potential to build an enormous back-end sales annuity.

In this section we're going to give you several examples of how to mine your back-end if you have the type of business that has an automatic one. And we're also going to show you how to develop a great back-end even if your business doesn't, by it's own nature, have one.

After all, you do want to cash in on this huge annuity, don't you?

Notice that we said annuity.

That's because once you develop and religiously work your back-end, these additional sales will virtually turn into an annuity that could pay you far more than the total of all of your front-end sales.

OK, you're probably getting real excited by now, but let's take this one step at a time.

First, here's why working your back-end is so incredibly profitable.

It costs you a significant amount of money to find and generate a new customer.

We already covered this, but let's take another look at it.

Suppose you run a promotion that costs you $5,000. And suppose that promotion brings in 100 new customers.

That means that your new customer acquisition cost is $50.

In other words, it costs you $50 dollars to generate each new customer.

If you run a business with an automatic back-end, you now know that by simply taking good care of that customer, he or she will come back and buy again and again.

And each time that customer comes back to buy, you are already ahead by that $50 that you didn't need to spend in marketing costs to find him.

That's one reason that the back-end is frequently more profitable than the front-end, but let's look at it a little deeper.

In fact, let's apply "*The Lost Art Of Common Sense*" to it.

Since you delivered great customer service, and built a high degree of credibility and trust in the customer's mind, you know that the customer is already predisposed to do business with you again.

In fact, anytime he or she thinks of your product or service, he or she thinks of you, right?

Why not make them think of your product or service more often?

That's what we call *working* the back-end.

Instead of merely waiting for your customers to come back and do more business with you, give them an irresistible reason to come in right now and buy something.

Hey, we're really on to something here.

But before you can tell your customers an irresistible reason to come in right now and make another purchase, you have to know who they are.

Which leads us to the first "*common sense rule*" for developing and working your back-end.

It's very simple.

Get every customers name, address, and phone number! Start doing it right now.

This is, quite frankly, the most valuable information that you could ever imagine.

In fact, it's the key to your "*pot of gold!*"

It's the only way you can effectively market your back-end to your existing customers.

After all, you do need to know who you want to "*talk*" to, don't you?

Most businesses don't yet collect this information. Some of them collect it, but then do nothing with it. In fact, many of the ones that do collect it, actually throw it away.

What a shame. That's like throwing away buckets full of money!

If you sell by mail, or if you deliver your products or services to your customers, then you are already collecting this important information.

If you sell at retail, and your products are high-ticket items with warranties, again, you are probably already collecting this information.

But suppose you don't have the kind of business that is routinely collecting customer names, addresses, and phone numbers.

If that's the case, try one or more of the following techniques.

First, let's look at the obvious...

Simply have your sales people *ask the customer* for their names and addresses.

They should tell the customer that you frequently come across special buys that you can't get in enough quantity to advertise to the general public.

But that you hate to turn these incredible opportunities down, so you generally send a special bulletin to your preferred customers so they can take advantage of these unbelievable deals.

Then give the customer an appealing example.

Maybe you are working on a closeout purchase of a product that would go well with what the customer just bought.

Or perhaps you're trying to negotiate a special program for something that the customer has already indicated that he or she would be interested in buying in the future.

Here's another way to collect your customer names and addresses...

You could take our suggestion from the fifth *secret, "The Value Of A Good Education",* and start a newsletter.

Explain the value of this newsletter to your customers and offer to set them up with a complimentary subscription.

Make sure to tell the customer about some of the things that you'll cover in the newsletter. Tell them how they'll learn how to get so much more value, fun, utility, and profit from learning the information in the newsletter.

Another way to collect your customer names and addresses is to set your stores up as payment centers for customers to drop off their phone or utility bills.

Here's one of our favorite ways to get customer names and addresses...

Have a monthly drawing for a valuable prize. Do this by putting up an attractive display, and promote the giveaway to your customers.

Make sure the prize carries enough of a perceived value to entice most of your customers to fill out a card with their name, address, and phone number.

On a monthly basis, hold the drawing, and notify the winner.

Since we're discussing your back-end, here's how to immediately cash in on the drawing.

Write a letter to everyone who entered the drawing that month and *didn't* win the grand prize.

If you owned a restaurant, here's an example of what you should say.

Dear Mrs. Smith,

Thank you for entering our drawing last month.

Unfortunately, you didn't win the grand prize. That was won by Lucky Louie.

However, you did win a valuable 2nd prize. Simply come in for dinner within the next 30 days, and I'll buy dessert for every member of your party.

We really appreciate your patronage, and this bonus prize is just one way that we can thank you for your support.

Another way is to guarantee that every time you visit us, we'll always provide you with a delicious, satisfying meal and impeccable service, all for a very reasonable price.

Thank you again, and bon appetite,

Warmly,

Chef Brad

P.S. I look forward to seeing you soon, and please accept these FREE desserts with my compliments.

Of course, you might not own a restaurant. You might have a sporting goods store.

If that were the case, you'd simply change the letter to say something like...

Dear Mr. Smith,

Thank you for entering our drawing last month.

Unfortunately, you didn't win the grand prize. That was won by Lucky Louie.

However, you did win a valuable 2nd prize. I'd like to invite you to attend our exclusive golf clinic featuring pro golfer Sammy Slicer. It's going to be held at the Green Valley Golf Course from 10:00 A.M to 5:00 P.M on Sunday, June 12, 1992.

This clinic normally costs $49, and sells out as soon as it's announced. That's why we only make it available to our most cherished customers.

And I'd like you to attend as my guest.

That's right, you may attend this valuable clinic absolutely FREE.

We really appreciate your patronage and this bonus prize is just one way that we can thank you for your support.

Another way is to guarantee that every time you visit us, we'll always provide you with the best selection of quality sporting goods and expert advice and service, all for a very reasonable price.

Thank you again, and have a good game.

Warmly,

Alan J. Antin

P.S. I look forward to having you as my special guest. After this important golf clinic, you should be able to quickly take several strokes off your game.

Of course, at the golf clinic, you can pretty much count on selling some clubs, balls, private lessons, golf clothing, or club-fitting services.

Try this "FREE drawing" technique. Just modify the letters to fit *your* business. It should work wonders for you.

Whatever method works best for you, use it religiously to get those names and addresses.

It really is important. In fact, it's vital to your success.

But make sure you do it honestly and ethically, otherwise the "bad will" that you'll create will negate any gain from the use of this information.

Ok, so now that you have your customers' names and addresses, how do you properly use this information?

Well, again, the answer is painfully obvious...

Market to your existing customers the same way you marketed to get them to become customers in the first place.

Start writing to your customers... often.

Very often. In fact, you should communicate to your customers every 3-5 weeks.

And every time you communicate with your customers, you should re-explain all of the wonderful things that you do for them and rekindle those warm feelings that they have for you.

Then describe another wonderful product or service that would work perfectly for them...

And ask them for more money!

That's it in a nut-shell.

If you have a restaurant, it's dirt simple.

Invite them to come back and sample a special new entree, or offer them a FREE dessert, or bottle of wine with dinner.

If you are a dry cleaner, invite them to bring in their drapes for a special cleaning at an attractive price, or tell them about your special leather cleaning service, or invite them to participate in a special monthly "bulk cleaning" deal.

Maybe you'll find that you could offer a service to your regular customers whereby they can bring in all of the clothes they want cleaned, as often as they want, for a flat monthly fee.

What a great way to lock them into an ongoing, and extremely profitable relationship.

If you sell any kind of service that customers use (or should use) on a fairly regular basis, you should try a "*continuity*" program. By this we mean simply set your customers up on a special deal that calls for you to automatically perform your service when required, and bill them each time.

OK, sign me up for the twelve month program.

Or, and this is even better, set them up on a "*TFN*" program with their credit card. That stands for Till Further Notice.

The way this works is that each month (or whatever period fits your business) you will automatically perform your service, or ship your product, and bill them on their credit card.

This goes on month after month until the customer cancels the arrangement.

Or, and this is even better still, offer them an even bigger discount to prepay a quarter's worth or a year's worth of your services.

The whole point is that you're locking up tons and tons of repeat business. In other words, building an automatic (and hugely profitable) back-end.

OK, so if you have the kind of business that gives you the ability to resell your customers either more of the same products and services, or additional products or services, you should write to (or call) them often, and continually solicit additional business.

Also, don't forget to try continuity and TFN programs.

And above all, don't be afraid to try any offer you think of. If it's an honest value, and if you present it properly, a large number of your customers are going to take you up on it.

Oh yes, just as a reminder, each of these communications (whether by phone or letter) should include all of the elements that you learned in the first seven *"secrets."*

Don't forget that even though they are already your customers, you still need to educate them...

You still need to give them the "reasons why"...

You still need to make them an irresistible offer...

You still need to use direct response techniques...

You still need to give them an *"Iron-Clad"* guarantee...

And you still need to *"service the hell out of them."*

But what do you do if you only sell one product or service, and your customers only purchase that product or service on a very infrequent basis?

Again, the solution can be found in common sense...

Find something else to sell them.

There are almost no rules here, so just look at some of these examples, and let your imagination run wild.

Suppose you sell high-end computer software that retailers would use to run their business.

So you typically market your software to small to mid sized-retailers. Let's further suppose that your software is at the higher end of the price range.

OK, you'll probably find that every time you run an advertisement or mail a sales letter to generate leads, a certain percentage of these leads will not be a correct fit for your software.

Perhaps their company is too big to use your system and they require a larger or more complex system.

Or, conversely, perhaps they don't need as complete and complex a system as the one you sell.

Well, most businesses would simply throw these prospects away.

But not you. You are tuned in to *"The Lost Art Of Common Sense Marketing."*

You know that each of these leads cost you money, and that someone else has the perfect product for these customers.

So you get on the phone, and call one of the companies that markets a cheaper software package and say something like...

"You know, Sam, the cost of getting new prospects in our business is getting to be quite high. And we all frequently get leads that our products simply won't work for.

"In fact, right now, I have about 50 prospects that simply can't use our software package. But, I believe your package would fit them to a tee.

"Why don't we work together and see if we can help these guys at the same time.

"Here's what I propose.

"A. We could sell each other our unusable leads for a fixed price.

"Or...

"B. We could turn over these leads to each other and agree that anytime one of them buys, we would pay each other a referral fee of

25%.

"Or...

"C. We could agree to actually endorse and even market each others products to these people on an even larger percentage split.

"The point is, Sam, that we are both investing a lot of money in these unusable prospects, and that by working together we can not only recoup money that otherwise would simply go down the drain, but we might even actually both profit substantially.

"What do you think?"

The key is to point out that the other guy has absolutely nothing to lose and everything to gain by making one of these deals with you, and you'll both profit nicely.

How's that for an unexpected "bonus" back-end?

Suppose you were a Realtor.

You may sell someone a new home only once every five to seven years (or even longer).

Here's how to develop a great back-end that could end up making you even more money per customer than your commissions.

Arrange a deal with dozens of companies that also serve the new home buyer market. Set it up such that you can make a special deal on their behalf to everyone to whom you sell a home.

Each time one of your home buyers makes an initial purchase from one of your suppliers, that supplier will pay you a percentage.

Think of all of the possibilities...

Furniture stores, interior decorators, landscapers, lawn services, pool services, plumbers, mechanics, home improvement companies, etc., etc.

The list could be endless.

Suppose you had a travel agency.

Go out and make a deal with a luggage supplier. Send a letter to all of your best clients that tells them about the fantastic deal you can get them on top quality luggage. Then split the profits with the supplier.

We could go on forever, but you get the point.

Once your customers are happy with you, continue to make them additional offers.

If you have the additional products or services already, great. If not, find other products or services and arrange to offer them to your customers.

They trust you and like you already, so they will be about 20 times more likely to buy from you than someone else.

That raises an important final caution.

Make absolutely certain that any "outside" products, or services that you endorse to your most valuable company asset (your customers), are provided by honest, ethical people, like you.

Make sure that your customers are treated as well by these *"joint-venture partners"* as they are by you. After all, they are *your customers*, and they're only buying based on the trust that you worked so hard to earn.

By now your head should be literally swimming with ideas for things you can sell to your customers.

That's good.

Write those ideas down before you forget them.

Now that you've discovered twelve of the *"secrets"* from *"The Lost Art Of Common Sense Marketing,"* go take a long hard look at your company.

You'll probably see dozens of ways to improve your marketing and cash in on the tide of change being instigated by today's *"vigilante consumers."*

Give them what they want, and they'll help you prosper. Ignore them, and your business will soon go the way of the dodo.

The twelve *"secrets"* that we've revealed here will lead you down the road of *"common sense marketing."* But it's up to you to begin the journey. We hope you do, and wish you all of the best.

Of course, we couldn't teach everything there is to know about the *"lost art"* in this one small book, but these basics should give you a wonderful (and profitable) start.

Now turn to the next (and final) section to learn how to discover the rest of *"The Lost Art Of Common Sense Marketing."*

Wrapping It All Up With A
Valuable, Unexpected, FREE Bonus!

You've now learned twelve very important "*secrets*" from "*The Lost Art Of Common Sense Marketing.*" Secrets that are the building blocks upon which to base your entire marketing foundation.

First, you discovered how the most valuable consultants in the world *(your own customers)* are free, and that if you simply ask them the right questions, they'll reveal their unmet wants and desires.

Once you learn these unmet wants and start filling them, construct a strong Statement Of Benefit (S.O.B.). This S.O.B. tells the entire marketplace that you are meeting these wants and desires better than anyone else.

Always focus your advertising specifically to your best prospects in a way that makes them think that your message was written just for them.

And when you do "*talk*" to your prospects in your advertising, present a complete and compelling case for your offer, and do it in a way that practically forces them to respond immediately. Track the results so you'll know if your advertising is "*earning its keep.*"

Sometimes you need to put on your teacher's hat, and actually teach your prospects and customers how and why they should use your products and services.

Teach them well, and watch your sales sky-rocket.

And then, make them an incredible offer... an offer that's almost too good to be true, but tell them the reason why you're doing it. It builds credibility.

Don't forget to remove all of the perceived risk. When you show your prospects that you trust them, they're much more likely to trust you.

You now know that the only way to rate any advertising is to put it to a vote. And the only votes that count are when customers buy. Opinions of ads don't matter, results do.

Once you find the big winner, that *"killer ad,"* run it until another ad beats it. Even if it takes years. Different prospects are seeing your ad everytime. And if it's the best ad to sell your product this week, it's probably a good way to sell it next week.

Remember to also pay special attention to how a customer sees your business. Make it fun, easy, exciting, and convenient for them to trade with you.

And when they do deal with you, don't forget to reward them with the *"after dinner mint."* Make them feel special, and let them know how much you appreciate their support.

By using these *"secrets"* together as a complete foundation, you'll find the *"mother lode,"* and be able to upsell and resell your customers time after time after time.

Imagine what you could do if you also knew how to...

Grab even bigger chunks of market share from your competitors, and keep these new customers for life...

Write ads and sales letters that practically force your prospects to buy...

Make a fortune by actually *giving* your products away...

Mail a post card or letter to every single potential customer in your area -- ABSOLUTELY FREE!

When we finished writing this book, we gave advance copies to some of our friends, clients, and associates in order to get their comments and criticisms.

Boy were we surprised! The overwhelming majority of their comments dealt with their desire to learn more.

They practically demanded we teach them every bit of *"The Lost Art Of Common Sense Marketing"*

After all, there's so much more to learn.

And the secrets that we couldn't include in this short book are no less important and no less powerful than the twelve we did cover.

That's why we've launched a special new monthly newsletter called...

"The Antin Marketing Letter - Secrets From The Lost Art Of Common Sense Marketing"

In this unique, one-of-a-kind monthly marketing letter, we'll reveal to a select group of subscribers, virtually every secret... every technique... every concept... every method... and every single marketing strategy that we've ever discovered.

Each topic will be covered from the broad perspective all of the way down to the minute details. We'll leave no stone unturned, and no question unanswered.

Here's a quick preview of what you'll learn in addition to grabbing market share... writing killer sales pieces... giving products away for big profits... and mailing free...

How to turn marginal promotions into winners and winning promotions into homeruns...

How to use cheap little classifieds to attract new customers like a bear is attracted to honey...

A simple method that forces your prospect to open AND READ your sales letter...

How to turn your dead inventory into cash almost overnight...

How to apply principles, that not one in a hundred ad agencies know, to craft an ad that will pull in piles of money and new customers...

How to place an ad in almost any newspaper or magazine for a fraction of what most people pay, and sometimes with no up-front

181

cost at all...

A super secret technique for yellow page advertising that almost guarantees the prospect will call you instead of your competitors...

How to create powerful, valuable bonus products that cost you nothing, but that your customers would pay dearly for...

How to "*train*" your customers to buy more from you and do it more often...

How to profit from prospects that don't even buy from you...

How to use little premiums to upsell almost any customer...

How (and when) to use "*teaser*" copy to boost response. Do it wrong, and your mail ends up in the dumpster...

These are just a few of the things you'll learn from...

"The Antin Marketing Letter - Secrets From The Lost Art Of Common Sense Marketing"

You can't learn them in any school, college, or university... and you can't learn them from any of those "*get-rich-quick*" books and seminars.

Of course, we certainly practice what we teach, so you can bet that we've come up with an absolutely irresistible way for you to sample "The Antin Marketing Letter - Secrets From The Lost Art Of Common Sense Marketing."

Remember how we said that the best way to build credibility and trust with the prospect is to actually reverse the risk, rather than simply try to reduce it?

Well, try this on for size...

We'd like to give you a little gift to help you along your journey towards discovering all of the "Lost Art Of Common Sense Marketing."

We'd like to give you a FREE, bonus, trial subscription to "The Antin Marketing Letter - Secrets From The Lost Art Of Common

Sense Marketing."

And, as you can imagine, we've made it extremely easy for you to get your subscription started...

Simply call toll free, 1 (800) 442-4249 right now and ask for it. We'll immediately rush the current issue to you via first class mail. Then, you'll receive the next two issues at the same time as our regular subscribers.

All together, you'll get three complete jam-packed profit producing issues absolutely FREE. Now, pick up the phone and call right now, before you forget. The phone is answered 24 hours a day, seven days a week. The call is absolutely FREE, and so is the trial subscription. The toll free number is 1 (800) 442-4249.

When you subscribe to "The Antin Marketing Letter - Secrets From The Lost Art Of Common Sense Marketing," you'll become privy to the most formidable, powerful, and profitable business strategies known to man. And your competitors will never know what hit them.

We hope you enjoyed this book, and would appreciate you writing down any comments or criticisms you may have and sending them to us at the following address.

**The Antin Marketing Group, Inc.
600 Cleveland Street, Suite 780
Clearwater, Florida 34615
Telephone (813) 468-2000
FAX (813) 446-4381**

For additional copies of this book send check to the above address:

> 1 - 5 copies - $14.95 each
> 6 - 24 copies - $9.95 each
> 25 or more copies - $6.95 each

Please add $3 for shipping and handling for the first book and $1 for each additional book. For 25 or more books, we pay shipping.

Acknowledgements

We'd like to thank the many people who have generously given us their time, talent, expertise, and opinions for the completion of this book.

We owe them a debt of gratitude.

Sara Antin

Sidney Antin

Joan Bowen

Dan Compton

Tammi Crotteau

Loretta Duffy

Debra Filla

Jim Fry

Dick Guyer

Doug Guyer

Gary Halbert

Bill Hammond

John Kremer

Bill Myers

Karen Myers

Ted Nicholas

Srikumar Rao